D0113248

SUNDAY HOMILIES

SUNDAY HOMILIES

CYCLE A

Herbert F. Smith, SJ

ALBA · HOUSE   NEW · YORK

SOCIETY OF ST. PAUL, 2187 VICTORY BLVD., STATEN ISLAND, NEW YORK 10314

Library of Congress Cataloging-in-Publication Data

Smith, Herbert F.
    Sunday homilies: the "A" cycle / Herbert F. Smith.
        p.   cm.
    ISBN 0-8189-0560-3
    1. Church year sermons.   2. Catholic Church — Sermons.
    3. Sermons, English.   I. Title.
    BX1756.S595S86   1989
    252'.6 — dc20
                                  89-32895
                                  CIP

Imprimi Potest
James A. Devereux, S.J.

Nihil Obstat
Sidney C. Burgoyne
Censor Librorum

Imprimatur
† Anthony J. Bevilacqua
Archbishop of Philadelphia
April 20, 1989

Designed, printed and bound in the United States of
America by the Fathers and Brothers of the
Society of St. Paul, 2187 Victory Boulevard,
Staten Island, New York 10314, as part of their
communications apostolate.

Printing Information:

Current Printing - first digit 1 2 3 4 5 6 7 8 9 10 11 12

Year of Current Printing - first year shown
1989   1990   1991   1992   1993   1994   1995   1996

CONTENTS
Cycle A

Preface ix
1st Sunday of Advent
  The Meaning of Advent 3
ABC — Immaculate Conception
  The Lowly Lifted — Mary's Story 6
2nd Sunday of Advent
  This Waiting Is Work 9
3rd Sunday of Advent
  Imitating Him We Excel 12
4th Sunday of Advent
  Tragedies Into Triumph 15
ABC — Christmas Vigil Mass
  The God-Man's Own Love Story .17
ABC — Mass on Christmas Day
  The Day of Our Happiness 20
Holy Family
  Healing the Family 24
ABC — Solemnity of Mary, Mother of God
  Mother of the Highest and the Lowest 27
ABC — Epiphany
  Christian Faith for the World 30
Baptism of the Lord
  This Mysterious Baptism 33
2nd Sunday of the Year
  Jesus' Baptism and Ours 36
3rd Sunday of the Year
  The Meaning of Life 39

4th Sunday of the Year
Moral Living on a New Plateau .... .42
5th Sunday of the Year
The Morality That Attracts .... .45
6th Sunday of the Year
The Higher Law of Christ .... .48
7th Sunday of the Year
Messianic License .... .52
8th Sunday of the Year
Putting Money in Its Place .... .55
1st Sunday of Lent
Secrets of the Dying and Rising of Christ .... .58
2nd Sunday of Lent
The Steep Climb to Sanctity .... .61
3rd Sunday of Lent
Saved by the "Enemy" .... .64
4th Sunday of Lent
Ending All the Darkness .... .68
5th Sunday of Lent
No Waiting For Life .... .71
Passion (Palm) Sunday
A Week With Christ .... .74
ABC — Easter Sunday
Eastering With Jesus .... .77
2nd Sunday of Easter
Yeshua Yahweh .... .80
3rd Sunday of Easter
Recognizing Jesus .... .83
4th Sunday of Easter
Where are the Yearling Shepherds? .... .86
5th Sunday of Easter
Deacons Restored .... .90
6th Sunday of Easter
God's Own Truth .... .93
Ascension
A New Game Plan for Life .... .96

Contents

vii

7th Sunday of Easter
Companions of God 99
ABC — Pentecost Sunday
Lovers' Guide 102
Trinity Sunday
The Family God 105
Corpus Christi
The Real Presence 107
ABC — St John the Baptist
If John the Baptist Were Here 112
ABC — Solemnity of SS Peter and Paul, Apostles
Praising Our Faith's Founding Fathers 115
13th Sunday of the Year
In the Beginning, Baptism 118
14th Sunday of the Year
The Sacrament of Christ's Compassionate Heart 121
15th Sunday of the Year
Faith We Can Depend On 124
16th Sunday of the Year
The Book 127
17th Sunday of the Year
The Living Gospel 130
18th Sunday of the Year
Hunger No More 133
19th Sunday of the Year
Help Beyond Hope 137
ABC — Assumption
Mary the Model Christian 140
20th Sunday of the Year
Calling All Nations! Calling All Nations! 143
21st Sunday of the Year
Christ, Peter and the Pope 146
22nd Sunday of the Year
Summons to Suffering 150
23rd Sunday of the Year
Giving and Receiving Correction .153

24th Sunday of the Year
   The Mature Christian's Forgiving Heart 156
25th Sunday of the Year
   Attitudes of the Mature Christian 159
26th Sunday of the Year
   How To Be a Good Catholic 163
27th Sunday of the Year
   Proud Guardians of Life 166
28th Sunday of the Year
   Anticipating Heaven's Joy 169
29th Sunday of the Year
   One Billion Missionaries 172
30th Sunday of the Year
   Made For Love . . . . :176
ABC — Feast of All Saints
   Home to the Father 179
31st Sunday of the Year
   Overcoming Our Crisis of Faith 182
32nd Sunday of the Year
   How To Prepare For Death 185
33rd Sunday of the Year
   The Mandate To Excel 189
34th Sunday of the Year: Christ the King
   Our King's Law of Love 192

PREFACE

"Giving a homily is a personal affair." True. "Preparing a homily is an objective affair." Also true, and the reason this book can be useful as a source of homily material. Homilies should be personal, an outflow of the giver's own religious faith, convictions and passion. But they should also deliver the objective Good News as found in Scripture and taught in the Church.

So highly personal was Archbishop Sheen's delivery that they used to say he had trouble deciding whether to become a priest or an actor, and settled it by becoming an actor. So faithful were his homilies to the Gospel and the Church that their usefulness has outlasted his earthly sojourn.

PREPARING A HOMILY

To modify an old bridal aphorism, a homily should be composed of "something old, something new, something borrowed, and something of you."

The *old* is the inspired word of God, the foundation and substance of the homily. The word of God is timelessly old, and fresher than tomorrow. Our task is to make its inexhaustible newness flash out. To make familiar Scripture more familiar is to pass the congregation a soporific. It is necessary to make it unfamiliar; it is also possible. We do it by exposing its inscape and its landscape, its deepest, mystical meaning, and its unbounded meaning for all time.

The *new* lies in its connection with the here and now. Finding it takes thought and study. It keeps us alert for some current event that, by its unstrained connection with the Gospel, will draw people from the secular to the sacred.

The *something borrowed* is where these homilies bow in. Another preacher's insights and research can broaden our grasp of the Gospel event. We avoid impersonalism and plagiarism not by refusing to borrow, but by adding our own headwork and prayer. As the fundamentalist preacher said, "I reads myself full, thinks myself straight, prays myself hot, and then lets fly!"

Preaching is a heavy responsibility. Busy priests need all the help they can get. One parish priest wrote to me: "Whenever your homilies appear in *Homiletic Review,* I have found them after my own heart. I enjoy them and find them most helpful in preparing and delivering my own Sunday homilies here in a busy parish." He wanted to know if more were available. This book is my answer.

A National Opinion Research Center poll found young Catholics more attuned to and affected by parish sermons than by encyclicals. Good preaching helps them feel close to the Church and the parish. That's a motive to give the best, most authentic homilies we can.

The *something of you* is the personal element. I once watched a Billy Graham program with the question, "Why is Billy so effective?" I soon learned one reason: He or his guests gave powerful personal testimonial to their discovery of Christ. About the same time, I attended an Alcoholics Anonymous meeting. I felt the power of those who witnessed to how hellish it was when they were under the influence, how free they were made by a Power greater than themselves, and how it is now to be gloriously sober. In that same season, perusing the Acts of the Apostles, I read with opened eyes how Christianity in the beginning spread by the force and eloquence of that same kind of personal witness, given by intimates of Jesus. A sentence or two about one's own religious experience, especially if it is humbling, can make a homily pulse with intimacy and life.

A HOMILY PREPARATION TECHNIQUE

Many of the homilies in this book were composed as follows: Early in the week I read next Sunday's Gospel, and let gestation begin. Once alerted, I find verses flashing out from the scriptural passages in the Mass and the Office. In the course of the week, I read and outline the Proper, and probe for the theme. The Opening Prayer always helps. Next, I keep my eye on the news of the week for a point of contact with a current event.

Very useful is the "Pastoral Homiletic Plan" published by the *Homiletic and Pastoral Review* (Aug.-Sept., 1979). It proposes a theme for each Sunday, to help us cover more systematically the key points of Catholic doctrine and life. Without letting it confine us, we can use it to deepen our homilies and widen our nets.

As the week proceeds I begin outlining the homily in the form of Introductory Story, Three Key Points, and Concluding Remarks. This mental filing cabinet organizes the homily and plants it in the memory. I consult exegetical works as needed, and do other suited reading. This process is simple and effective. It produces a far better homily than the same amount of time invested at one sitting.

In the Sunday penitential rite, I say "Let us call to mind our sins, especially" — and I give the Gospel theme as I will treat it. This helps the people tune in better to the readings.

THE NATURE OF A GOOD HOMILY

What makes a homily good? There is fundamental disagreement today. You'll find articles claiming the genuine homily doesn't seek to catechize or convert to Gospel values or exhort to virtue. It rather moves the people to praise and celebration, by showing from the day's Gospel that God is continuing the same work of salvation in our lives. The weak doctrinal and moral content that has resulted from errors such as this has been pointed out in high Church circles, and steps are being taken to remedy it.

The *New Catholic Encyclopedia* traces the history of the homily. Quotes from the Fathers indicate that their homilies explained and applied the scriptural teaching, and exhorted inert listeners to action. Origen says a popular exegesis was given, not a learned lesson. The pedantic approach was shunned, but not teaching. They tried to inspire by using "the examples of the saints and mystical explanations." Extant patristic homilies confirm this explanation.

MAGISTERIAL GUIDANCE FOR THE HOMILY

The Constitution on the Sacred Liturgy says the sermon "should draw its content mainly from scriptural and liturgical sources, for it is the proclamation of God's wonderful works in the history of salvation, which is the mystery of Christ ever made present and active in us, especially in the celebration of the liturgy" (35). Number 52 amplifies this directive: "By means of the homily the mysteries of the faith and the guiding principles of the Christian life are expounded from the sacred text during the course of the liturgical year."

The Third Instruction on the Correct Implementation of the Sacred Liturgy (1970) provides this succinct directive: "The purpose of the homily is to explain the readings and make them relevant for the present day." *The General Catechetical Directory* amplifies this point. "It is necessary for the ministry of the word to set forth the divine revelation such as it is taught by the Magisterium, and such as it expresses itself, under the watchful eye of the Magisterium, in the living awareness and faith of the people of God. In this way, the ministry of the word is not a mere repetition of ancient doctrine, but rather it is a faithful reproduction of it, with adaptation to new problems and with a growing understanding of it."

The 1967 *Instruction on the Worship of the Eucharistic Mystery* declares that pastors should show the faithful "the close connection between the liturgy of the Word and the celebration of the Lord's Supper, so they can see clearly how the two constitute a single act of worship." And so "it is the purpose of the liturgy of the Word to develop the close connection between the preaching and hearing of the Word of God and the eucharistic mystery."

The current Canon Law, numbers 762-9, officially summarizes what is required of the homilist. Here is its gist: Priests are to value preaching greatly. Proclaiming the Gospel is among their principal tasks. It is the living word of God that brought the people together. The homily is the preeminent form of preaching. It is part of the liturgy, and "in the homily the mysteries of the faith and the norms of Christian living are to be expounded from the sacred text throughout the course of the liturgical year."

In summary: The homily presents an exposition of the scriptural text of the day. It connects the divine Word with the Eucharistic mystery, the feast of the day, the Scriptures as a whole, the doctrine of the Church, and the lives and needs of the worshippers. It should inform, form, reform, and inspire the faithful to believe, celebrate, and live the Good News.

The typical seven-minute homily is too short to do the job these texts set before us. It tallies to about four hours of preaching a year — less than a minor course in school. It deprives the people of the necessary guidance in a complex society, and the inspiration and exhortation needed to survive in a secularized society.

DOCTRINAL HOMILIES AND THE CRISIS OF FAITH

These homilies attempt, in harmony with the readings, to speak firmly about faith and doctrine and the moral life. We need to recall that Jesus spoke his truths whether convenient or inconvenient, welcome or unwelcome, even to the point of saying to the Twelve, "Do you also want to go away?"

Objection is made that people want their consciences respected. They should be respected, by teaching the Church's doctrine on conscience, without omitting its doctrine on the obedience of faith due the magisterium. The faithful in turn must respect the conscience of the priest, who is charged by ordination to preach unblemished the word of God as understood and believed in the Church.

There is a Jewish story about a holy rabbi who wept bitterly as death approached. His surprised nephew sung his merits, concluded with the fact that he never sat in judgment against others, and asked why he wept. The rabbi replied, "That is why I weep: I was given the ability to establish justice, but never carried it out."

THE COURAGE TO PREACH

We in the West are fortunate. We have the freedom to preach the truth. We need but the courage. Christian preaching is prophetic. It demands much courage. The homilist who preaches as he ought loses congregants; the one who does not, loses himself.

"Pastors who lack foresight," wrote St. Gregory the Great, "hesitate to say openly what is right because they fear losing the favor of men. As the voice of truth tells us, such leaders are not zealous pastors who protect their flock, rather they are like mercenaries who flee by taking refuge in silence when the wolf appears." And he adds, "The Lord reproaches them through the prophet: 'They are dumb dogs that cannot bark.' " St. Augustine says, "I dare to say, 'You wish to stray, you wish to be lost; but I do not want this.' For the one whom I fear does not want this . . . shall I fear you rather than him?"

Fr. Louis Bourdaloue, praised as one of the great preachers, gave a blunt sermon in the presence of King Louis XIV, who was no model Christian. The court spoke critically of the preacher, but the king retorted, "Fr. Bourdaloue has done his duty; let us do ours." One wit commented, "Fr. B. charges highly in the pulpit, but he sells cheaply in the confessional." That is the right spirit.

We have many guidelines for preaching. Here is a unifying principle: Preach Jesus and his Gospel in fidelity to the Church, and in ways that bind the hearts of the faithful to the Heart of Christ. Millions drift into fundamentalism when not introduced to a personal, intimate relationship with Jesus. If we effectively preached the most intimate relationship of all, that with the risen Jesus in Holy Communion, could they ever be pried away?

HOLDING ATTENTION

Short homilies are preferred by many people. But lack of spiritual hunger is a concern, not an excuse. When loved ones are not eating, we coax them to take nourishment, and try to find foods that promote health and stimulate the appetite.

There is no easy way to capture attention. Prayer-found fervor and sensitivity to people's concerns work best. We should pepper our homilies with illustrations from family life, and illustrate the rewards of holiness by showing what it can do for family happiness. Mention of family concerns perks up attention — for good reason. God is a family in heaven, and became a member of one on earth, and he made us in his image and likeness.

A good literate style gets attention, but over-brilliance attracts to the preacher rather than to Christ's message. Christ's own word has the appeal of form as well as content. Homilies should have brief passages of beauty, so listening is its own reward; and insights, so even the learned will never have seen things quite this way; and the challenge which is inherent in the word of God, that stings and wakes even the inattentive.

We should never read homilies. The living word is too powerful to neglect. Its fluidity evokes attention; it leaves room for the Holy Spirit. Literary finesse is lost, but the loss can even be beneficial. Finesse appeals to the aesthetic sense. We are out to move more than the aesthetic sense, and more than mountains. We are out to move minds to faith. We are out to move hearts to God.

CYCLE A

THE MEANING OF ADVENT

We Christians await the second coming of the Messiah, but the Jews who do not accept Jesus tell the following tale to hint at why the Messiah hasn't come: The Messiah, waiting in eternity for the right time, has pity on a devout Jew and comes and says, "Here, take this little black bag. Reach in whenever you need anything; and if an enemy comes, swallow him up in the black bag." From that day, the man became wealthy and forgot about God until the Angel of Death called. Terrified, the man held out the black bag and swallowed up the Angel of Death. The Messiah came to give him a stern lecture but the man held out the black bag and swallowed up the Messiah too. And the story ends, "Now do you know why the Messiah hasn't come?" We Christians might say, "Now do you know why the Messiah hasn't returned?" Jesus is saying something similar in today's Gospel. People not prepared don't want his return.

This first Sunday of Advent and first day of the new Liturgical Year gives us a fresh chance to prepare for his final coming.

We speak of three comings of Christ. His first coming was his birth on that first Christmas. Next, he came into our lives by faith and the Church. And last will be his final coming, to end our trials and gather us to him in glory.

Let's look at the obstacles to Christ's coming, at how to prepare for Christmas, and at how to give Christ our hearts.

First, we look at the obstacles to Christ in our lives. Did you notice anything strange about the obstacles to God in the life of those who died in the flood? They were eating, drinking, and marrying. What's wrong with that? It compels us to ask, "But what was their mortal sin?'' Our Lord is making us think. All he says about their sin is this: ''They were totally unconcerned.'' Unconcerned about what? About God, of course. About God who created them for himself, to love and be loved. Their mortal sin was materialism. They chose this life over life with God. The first commandment says, ''You shall not have strange gods before me'' — not the gods of materialism, not the gods of life in this world. There is nothing wrong with eating and drinking and marrying, unless it is set above adoration of God. If challenged, they probably would have said, ''Hey, what's wrong with my life?'' And God answered with the flood.

This is the chief danger for most — living a secular, materialistic life which puts God second. Statistics show that 50 percent of Catholics are not at Mass on Sundays. God did not say, ''Half of you keep the Sabbath Day holy,'' or ''Keep half the Sabbath Days holy.'' That irreligious attitude is what Jesus is condemning.

Think of the world's preparation for Christmas — its use of Christmas decorations and songs in a merely cultural way. It is beautiful to see the Christmas lights and scenes in the Advent twilight even in the stores. But let us shun the secular meaning of preparing for fun and gifts on Christmas, instead of for Christ.

If we put anything before the Lord, there are always telltale signs. We don't have time for Sundays. We don't have time to pray. We may not even have time to keep the Lord's commandments.

How, then, do we as true Christians prepare for Christmas? One beautiful practice is to attend Mass daily; if not daily, then some days. It can change your life. One young man began to long for daily Mass, but didn't go because he didn't want to be thought of as a ''Holy Joe.'' At last he saw his cowardice and overcame it, and went on to the priesthood too. Is it bad to be a ''Holy Joe'' like St. Joseph?

Meditate on the Gospels and the birth of Jesus. In the first reading, Isaiah prophesied that people would stream to Jerusalem from all over the world. We do it by faith every time we gather and worship Christ, and every time we take the Bible and meditate.

In the second reading St. Paul exhorts us to redouble our fight against sin, mindful that our salvation is getting closer. We have to stop any carousing, sexual excess, quarreling or jealousy. Work to get rid of any other sins as well. There is always further to go to "put on Christ," as Paul said even about himself. One of the great ways to "put on Christ" is to grow in affection for Christ's members, with first regard for those in our own family.

One of the most blessed things we can do is be a peacemaker. Start small. Begin by cultivating peace in your own heart. When we have it, we radiate it, people sense it. Join some organization that promotes peace and order. Work for Right to Life. Abortion destroys innocent life and brings unrest to the whole land. This season, in which we recall the Son of God living as an embryo in his mother's womb, certainly invites us to reverence for life. A contribution to peace is a beautiful birthday gift to the Prince of Peace.

Finally, how can we give our hearts to Christ? Begin by recalling that Christianity is not so much something as Someone. It's Christ and us. We are his members, he is our life and our future resurrection. That is Christianity. It is life with God and new life from God. And that is where our love and our hearts should be — with Jesus. So during this Advent season, try to focus your prayer and attention on Jesus, not just in moments of formal prayer, but always. Call to him to come more deeply into your life. He wants to live with us not only day in and day out, but hour by hour. On the last evening with us, when he gave the Eucharist which we celebrate here, he said, "Anyone who loves me will be true to my word, and my Father will love him; we will come to him and make our dwelling place with him." That's the heart of all prayer. We don't have to shout to be heard.

Long for Jesus in Holy Communion. He is your life; you, his

body. Ask the Virgin Mary to feed you on her very substance, the Son of her womb. Ask Jesus to help you find him living in you and in all his members, so your love will grow.

How many of us have ever said seriously, "I'm called to be a saint"? It *is* our call. Jesus called us to become perfect like our heavenly Father. Have the courage to look at yourself as God wants you to be, and say, "Lord Jesus, I'm going to quietly get to work at it." Every step of the way is a giving of your heart to Christ.

Let us move on now to offer our sacrifice of Jesus to the Father, and to receive him into our bodies and our hearts in Holy Communion. There can be no better preparation for his birthday.

"ABC" — Immaculate Conception

Gn 3:9-15, 20
Ep 1:3-6, 11-12
Lk 1:26-38

THE LOWLY LIFTED — MARY'S STORY

A young girl in a small town was once visited unexpectedly by a most striking guest. He praised her so lavishly it frightened her. The visit took place some 2,000 years ago, the girl was Mary, and the guest, the Archangel Gabriel.

A modern pilgrim to the Holy Land gazed in shock at the little cave-like dwelling identified as what remains of Mary's home, and whispered in shock, "I thought she was the daughter of kings!" The Gospels actually tell us little of Mary's lineage, but the tradition in the Church does recall her descent from King David. And the Gospels do tell us that Joseph was of the line of David. That is why he went to Bethlehem, the town of David, to register for the census. David, however, reigned a thousand years before, and the last of his line was dethroned some 500 years prior to Joseph's birth. So it is no surprise that Joseph's royal ancestry seems to have brought him no power or wealth or prestige.

Mary and Joseph were poor. They lived in the unpretentious town of Nazareth, perched on a mountaintop in Galilee, home of some 500 rustic souls. Sophisticated Jerusalemites thought of Galileans as a rude, uncultured people. Nazarenes were considered a cut worse. Nathanael, himself a Galilean, said, "Can anything good come out of Nazareth?" Nazarenes were probably classified with the hillbillies of our day. One living Jewish writer does say a thing about Nazareth that reminds us of Mary. He says the women there have long had a reputation for beauty.

For 2,000 years now the world has joined the Angel Gabriel in praising the Blessed Virgin Mary. And though that unassuming girl was upset by the angel's praise, the world's praise would come as no surprise to her. For after the angel's visitation, she prophesied that "All generations will call me blessed." It was not her doing; it was "because he who is mighty has done great things for me." What are those great things?

Today we celebrate the first of them, her Immaculate Conception. Today's preface explains it when it confesses to God, "You allowed no stain of Adam's sin to touch the Virgin Mary." The sin of Adam is inherited by the rest of us together with his flesh, at our conception. It is not so with Mary. By the foreseen grace of her Son, the God-man, she was kept untouched by original sin, kept as innocent as he. The innocence he has by nature, she has by grace. As he is perfect Redeemer, she is the perfectly redeemed one. In Wordsworth's lovely phrase, she is "tainted nature's solitary boast." The innocence she received at conception, she kept forever. She is the new Eve, who said *no* to the seductive lies of that serpent, the devil.

Mary developed her gifts and matured, and became the perfect model of the religious person. Religion means dedication to God, which means doing always what pleases him, and Mary was obedient from the first. "Behold the handmaid of the Lord," she said. "Be it done to me as you say." Mary is also our perfect counselor. To us she said, "Do whatever he tells you." Ours is the age of the charismatic movement, and Mary is the charismatic woman above all others, the woman upon whom the Spirit descended in unmatched ways. She is the woman of prayer, who pondered God's marvels in her heart. She possesses the charism of virginity forever, along with the gift of motherhood, by a special favor of God.

All these gifts and many more are crowned by her greatest gift, the gift for which we untiringly sing her praise. She is the Mother of God's only Son, become Man in her by the overshadowing of the Holy Spirit. Her motherhood involves many more gifts. It filled her with such love that she never strayed from loving. Hers, we are told in the Opening Prayer, "is a love that never knew sin." She remained always true to herself, her love, her beloved.

Her motherhood also bestows on her the gift of joy. She is the joyous woman. What woman is completely happy who is not loved and fruitful, not bride and mother? Mary is bride of God and Mother of God. Who can ever know her joy?

Even this does not exhaust her virgin motherhood, for we have yet to recall her unique role in Salvation History, in God's plan for us all. By giving birth to Christ, our life, she is the new Eve, the true mother of all the living. She, the mother of us all, is even Mother of the Church and model of the Church.

What is our duty to such a mother? Ours is the joyous duty of sharing her holiness and happiness. The second reading tells us that God has "bestowed on us in Christ every spiritual blessing in the heavens." Does that not give us some share in Mary's title, "full of grace"? Paul says God has chosen us "to be holy and blameless," and to be "full of love." God gave us this blameless holiness in baptism, which is a kind of belated "immaculate conception." What we did not receive in our mother's womb, we received in the womb of the Church's baptismal font. By remaining faithful to our holiness as Mary did, we will share at our resurrection in her Assumption and heavenly glory.

We can never repay Mary, but let us at least pay her the honor of taking joy in her Immaculate Conception. It is in that joy that I close with a prayer of thanks to God for Mary.

Hail and blessed be the hour and the moment when that chaste married couple, Joachim and Ann, became parents. Blessed be that hour when they united in the act of married love, and conceived their daughter, Mary, and God, by his special favor, granted her an Immaculate Conception. Make that moment, O God, bring grace to all parents, and make the share in her holiness which we received at baptism bring us to share her glory with the Father, Son, and Holy Spirit forever. Amen.

"A" — Second Sunday of Advent
Is 11:1-10
Rm 15:4-9
Mt 3:1-12

THIS WAITING IS WORK

Advent is a time of waiting, but Advent waiting is a joy because we wait with assurance. After all, the Lord has already come by birth as man, is at present coming in mysterious ways, and will one day come again in visible majesty. And if that final coming has not occurred by Christmas, why then we have the joy of celebrating his birthday once again.

Waiting is a mixed experience — even the kind of waiting that is tinged with happy expectation. Take an inexperienced young salesman waiting for a client who could mean a major sale. He's anxious. He thinks, "Will my client show up? Will I make a good impression? Will he be satisfied with my product?"

We wait for Christ that way. He means more than money or success to us. He means salvation. Will we make a good impression on him when he arrives? Will he be satisfied with us, with our way of serving him? Will he accept us, take us into his kingdom?

John the Baptist told the people of his day they were not acceptable. They had to *reform*. The Greek word John uses for reform is
metanoia. Its literal meaning is *Change your mind!* Once we change
our mind in favor of God and his way, we feel remorse, sorrow, and
repentance for our former life, and we *turn* to God and his way. We
are *converted*. This is the process John the Baptizer is demanding. The
people were waiting passively for the Messiah. John said, *Wait by
reforming!* Do we need to reform if we are already converted? For an
answer, we turn to John and the Jewish people. John conceded they
were the children of Abraham — *but he warned that was not enough!*
Those were mere physical realities. Without the spiritual changes that
should go with them, the people would perish.

Jesus confirmed John. His first words in Mark's Gospel are,
"Reform your lives and believe in the Gospel." If Jesus spoke to
us today, what would he say? Would any of us be surprised if he
said, "Reform your lives and believe in the Gospel"?

We have to remember that reform is a process, the gradual
process of having our mind take on Christ's mind, and our heart
take on Christ's heart. The sacrament of penance is an important
part of this process. It belongs high on our Advent list. If possible,
we should attend an Advent Penitential Service. But don't think
Confession completes our Advent reform.

A look at the whole Church will point up what I mean. All the
members are baptized. Then why is God's reign not fully present?
The divisions in the Church make it evident it isn't. Contrast the
Church today with the vision of the peaceful society Isaiah says the
reign of God will usher in.

Where does this division come from except our failure to truly
reform? Is there not a gap between what the Gospels and the
Church teach, and what many Catholics hold? Catholics have not
undergone complete conversion, complete reform of every
worldly, or hard-hearted, or outrightly evil value. Beyond that,
isn't there a gap between what we believe and what we live —
between the heart of Jesus and our hearts?

There are three particular ways to work at our reform. The first is to fight against the worldliness that blocks out God — that makes us *too busy to wait for Christ*. Unless we succeed here, when Christ comes on Christmas, we will not be there. We may be in church, but our hearts won't be. Our hearts will be too wrapped up in our own affairs.

The second particular reform is to end our failure to be brothers and friends. Paul calls for this reform in today's second reading. And we can be sure of this — if we go to meet others more than half way, we will meet Christ on Christmas. We will even be meeting him on the way to Christmas, for he says, "What you do to others you do to me."

The third particular reform is to grow in love within our immediate family. In a way, all preparation for Christ consists in growing in love, and our family is always a good proving ground for love. Is there thoughtlessness to be corrected? Neglected responsibilities to be attended? Impatience to be overcome? Time to be made for family sharing? Any family member particularly neglected or in special need of attention? Any drifting of the family from Christ that needs reversing?

Is your house lacking prayer at meals, family recital of the rosary, religious pictures on the walls — at least a crucifix and an image of the Sacred Heart of Jesus? In brief, does the shape of your home and your lives lack what would mark you as the "domestic church" each Catholic family is meant to be?

If the answer to any of these questions is affirmative, won't you straighten it out for Advent? If all are affirmative, don't get disheartened; just get started. Any improvement shown by Christmas will be a gift and a promise of more that will be a pleasing Christmas present for Christ and your family.

I began with an example of waiting from the business world. I'll close with one from the affairs of the heart. A boy has a date. He is waiting for his girl when you happen to meet him. He tells you how much he's in love, and how anxiously he's waiting for his girl to show up. You're amazed, because his clothes are a disgrace, and he obviously needs a bath. You ask, "Don't you dress better than that for the girl you love?" He says, "Oh, I never thought about it. I always dress this way."

He ought to think about it, and so should we. We are to meet our God and Savior on Christmas. Let us think about the look of our souls and our lives — and do something about it for Advent.

"A" — Third Sunday of Advent

Is 35:1-6, 10
Jm 5:7-10
Mt 11:2-11

IMITATING HIM WE EXCEL

In a broad sense, the three important people today's Gospel is about are John, Jesus and you — John the forerunner, Jesus the trailblazer, and you his follower.

John's work is to point out the advent, the arrival, of Jesus. Since Christians celebrate Advent each year, John has been pointing out Jesus to Christians for 2,000 years, and is pointing him out to us today. He does it not by mere words, but by his life, and by the virtues that put backbone into his life.

If we are going to turn to Jesus as John did, and adhere to him through thick and thin as did John, we need the qualities John had. Let's look at those qualities through the eye of Jesus.

Jesus said of John, "What did you go out to see — a reed swaying in the wind?" Beside the Jordan river are hordes of tall reeds swaying with every wind. For 2,000 years since John, and despite him, hordes of Christians have swayed and bent with every wind of doctrine. John never swayed or bent. He lived unyielding and died a martyr. John was no reed. He was more like a giant California redwood!

John was a man of firmness, asceticism and commitment. In a word, he was a man of *discipline*. We live in an age full of reeds, but reeds cannot be faithful Christians. To be faithful to Christ, we have to be disciplined persons like John. Perhaps we can never be redwoods, but we can be tough, unbending little olive trees, committed to being true to our beliefs, rather than playthings of the winds of the world.

The word *discipline* is an interesting word. To some it conjures up an unpleasant picture of a rigid time order and a wooden personality. But that's only the way a reed looks at discipline, because to a reed anything with a backbone looks awfully stiff. The word *discipline* goes back to the Latin, and means both *information* and *formation*. For instance, the study of a subject is a discipline. But more importantly here, the word *discipline* means the depth of a person's intellectual formation, moral convictions, and faith. It was in this sense that John was disciplined, and Christ was disciplined. And we too must be disciplined to be faithful, to be rooted in the revelation and put forth the green leaves and the fruit of faith and morals, saying no to the world's invitation to drift in the backwaters of moral decay.

John was disciplined, but not rigid. He never showed the rigidity that fears the truth. He was fearlessly honest. Consider the event in today's Gospel, together with its background. Before being imprisoned, John had prepared the way for Christ, baptized him, and given witness that Jesus was the one who was to take away the sins of the world.

But then a terrible disappointment set in. The Jewish people expected the Messiah to sweep away foreign rule at once, and usher in the fabled age prophesied by Isaiah, the age we heard about in the first reading. John too probably had this expectation, but instead of things getting better for him, they got worse. Here he was imprisoned, helpless, in danger of death. If Jesus was really the Christ, why were things so bad? He sent his disciples to ask Jesus point blank whether he had made a mistake.

Jesus, too, was fearlessly honest. He told John's disciples simply to report what they saw and heard: the miracles foretold by Isaiah were being worked by him. The blind were seeing, the deaf hearing, the lame leaping about. But then Jesus added a dash of cold water. Blessed is the man who is not shocked by his lowly, peaceful ways, the man who does not reject him because he is being rejected by those who demand a warlord Christ.

Thus the theme of humility enters our reflections. Humility was part of John's backbone. He said of Jesus, "He must increase, I must decrease." He also said, "I'm not worthy to unlatch his sandal." We, too, need that kind of humility in order to imitate John in adhering to the lowly Jesus.

But then Jesus said two things about John that are not easily grasped. First, he said John was the greatest man born of woman. That makes John greater than all the prophets before him. That is surprising only until we examine the matter closely. Then we realize that the other prophets only foretold the Christ, but John pointed to him and said, *Here he is!* The second thing Jesus said about John was more mysterious. He said that each of us who has been born into the kingdom of God is greater than John. But if we look into this matter, we can understand it too. For John is the greatest man born of woman, but by baptism and the Holy Spirit, we were born of God. John had the spirit of prophecy, and could point out Christ, but we have the spirit of Christ, and therefore the grace to copy the Master whom John could only foreshadow.

During Advent we, like John, prepare ourselves and others for Christ's coming. We will please him when he comes on Christmas if we use Advent to copy John's discipline, honesty, and humility. For if we imitate John, we will come before Christ not only in the likeness of God the Father, which we received in baptism, but in the likeness of the greatest man born of woman. And that will carry us a long way toward being like Jesus, true God and true man.

"A" — Fourth Sunday of Advent   Is 7:10-14
Rm 1:1-7
Mt 1:18-24

TRAGEDIES INTO TRIUMPHS

Joseph and Mary are so prominently and dramatically featured in today's Gospel that we can miss its central focus. The central focus is on Jesus. Matthew himself makes that point in the lead sentence: "This is how the birth of Jesus Christ came about." Jesus, the lead actor, is still in Mary's womb, but he is the source and purpose of the drama. Not only today's Gospel passage, but every Gospel passage is at least indirectly about Christ. Paul makes this clear in today's second reading. "The Gospel of God," he writes, "the Gospel concerning his Son."

Mary and Joseph are servants of the Gospel, servants of Christ, preparing for his birth — preparing for Christmas, as we are. By examining their preparation, we can be helped in ours.

If we do not find our preparation easy, we may be consoled that Joseph found his a torment! It would be hard to find anywhere a more explosive passage than this account of Joseph's agony. He had become engaged to a virgin whose innocence he believed in beyond telling, and whose faithfulness he would have defended with his life. Yet here she was with child! Impossible! Her innocence and her pregnancy together shattered all logic! How could he deal with this situation, either logically or emotionally? If she had been raped, she would have told him. And if not, what had she done?

Mary saw Joseph's torment, and that made it her own. But what could she do? You don't tell a man you are pregnant by divine intervention. How could you ask a man to believe that simply on your word? No, the problem God had caused, God would have to solve. She was helpless.

There was a more pressing problem for Joseph than his

feelings. The Law called for the stoning of one who committed adultery — and the unfaithfulness of an engaged person was considered the same as adultery. Joseph was a man of God. He had to obey God's law. What was he to do? To his great credit, he solved the problem as best he could by not going beyond the facts. Mary was pregnant; he was not the father; he knew no more. Therefore, all he had to do was cancel the marriage.

If we tried to draw from the experience of Joseph and Mary a general religious principle, it might sound like this: *When God comes into our lives, we have trouble*. What is happening in their lives is that the great prophecy of Isaiah about the virgin giving birth to Emmanuel is being fulfilled — and that is what is causing his torment. The great event which Isaiah made to seem all joy is beginning for Joseph as all sorrow. In truth, this is simply the sign of the cross, which marks the life of Christ and of Christians. But what happens next in today's Gospel leads us to formulate our second principle: *When we have trouble, God comes*. God did come to Joseph, and explain to him the mystery, and Joseph took Mary home, and with her the Christ.

We too are brought to suffering and sometimes torment by fidelity to God's law, to the Church's teaching, to our commitments, to our loved ones. How often today the marriage vows, meant for joy, bring sorrow! But endurance brings a saved love, like Joseph's and Mary's. How often sex, meant for faithful love, brings on a pregnancy that seems intolerable. But what Joseph saw in Mary seemed intolerable to him, while it was in fact his eternal glory and the world's salvation. If Joseph lived in our day and asked for advice, isn't it likely that someone would have advised him to talk Mary into an abortion?

A college professor presented to his class the following problem: A man with syphilis had a tubercular wife who was pregnant. She had already borne four children: one was dead, the other three had an illness considered terminal. What should they do? Most of the students recommended abortion. The professor said, "Fine, you just killed Beethoven.'' Isn't that what the easy solution often does — kills what is most precious in our lives?

Married people and teenagers are not the only ones with problems. We all have problems. Priests too have their problems. For some, their priesthood is hard to bear, their celibacy is hard to live, so they quit, walk out. Is that a small thing? Not if you believe that through the priest's action the Holy Spirit brings to our altars the same Son of God he made incarnate in Mary's womb.

I have used a marriage problem, an unwanted pregnancy, a priest wrestling with his vocation, as examples of the struggles of us all. Whatever our problems or trials, the experience of Joseph and Mary is meant for us. It tells us that for people faithful to God, troubles are only the sign of the cross, which in Christ is the mark of the coming resurrection. If we believe that, we will imitate Joseph and Mary in being faithful to God and our loved ones, whatever our troubles. By this faithfulness, we will prepare and be prepared for Christ's birthday.

"ABC" — Christmas Vigil Mass

Is 9:1-6
Tt 1:11-14
Lk 2:1-14

THE GOD-MAN'S OWN LOVE STORY

The Christmas Vigil Mass readings report God's great journey into human flesh and blood, express the ardent love between him and us, and assure us that God is stronger than all our sins.

By tracing Jesus' ancestry, Scripture is tracing God's great journey into our flesh and blood. If each of us looked back into his own family tree, we'd make some interesting discoveries. Among the many good people, we'd very likely find horse thieves, adulterers and murderers.

Certainly, Jesus' own family tree is not lily white. It has its scoundrels. Even his ancestor, King David, a great saint and hero of his people, in moments of folly, was guilty of adultery and murder. Tamar, one of the mothers in his lineage, seduced Judah, one of the patriarchs. Ruth was a saintly pagan, and Rahab was at one time a prostitute. Yet it was from their flesh and blood that the Son of God was born.

What is God telling us then? That the worst follies and the worst sins cannot frustrate his plan; that he brings to goodness even the worst sinner who repents; and that he is not ashamed to join our human family despite its scandals.

Most of all, God is making it plain as the rising sun that he has taken hold of our flesh and blood just as it is, but without sin in him. His family tree is the story of his love pursuing us through the ages, preparing the way through his ancestors for his coming into the world. And he did come, and he became our flesh and blood, and that is what we celebrate. As Adam and Eve became one flesh by marriage, the Son of God became one flesh with human nature by his Incarnation in the womb of the Virgin Mary.

So we rejoice in the great love between God and us, despite the lovers' quarrels. In the reading from Isaiah the Lord tells us that he calls us his "Delight," and he promises, "As a young man marries a virgin, your builder" — that is, our Creator — "shall marry you." He has begun that mystical marriage by the Incarnation, and he has since carried it further. By the Incarnation he shared our human nature; by baptism he gave us a share in his divine nature; and in the Eucharist he unites himself to each one of us personally.

In the spiritual exercises of Advent the Church has been trying to get our sluggish love of God circulating in time for Christmas. Have you ever sat in one position for so long your leg fell asleep? We are the body of Christ, and if we don't return his love, it must be to him as though his leg were asleep — or worse, as though his heart were asleep.

This is the mystery of which we have become a part, and a timid love won't do. The Church is the bride of God living the most passionate love story of all. Our Holy Father, in his 1988 letter "On the Dignity and Vocation of Women," says that woman as virgin, bride and mother, is an image God has given us of how all of us should return love to the divine bridegroom. Of course, we have to take it spiritually. So we call Christ the bridegroom of our souls. Like a bride, we should be devoted to God; like a mother, we should bring forth spiritual "children," that is, good works. Is not that the way God himself speaks in the Scriptures?

The saints inspire us to this ardent love. The Psalmist says of God, "He is my love, my fortress; he is my stronghold, my Savior, my shield, my place of refuge." Here is a saint who speaks like a man of war, which he probably was — David wrote many of the psalms. And yet he is not so macho that he can't say in all simplicity, "God is my love." Do we have that kind of simplicity, and I must add, that kind of warrior's courage, to say, "God is my love"? The Psalmist says it, and is inviting us to say it; and, judging by his battle language, one who met him in person would soon be taught discretion if he flippantly rejected that invitation.

Jesus said, "Unless you become as little children, you cannot enter the kingdom of God." Jesus himself is inviting us to speak to God in all simplicity, like a little child, and say, "God, I love you."

We know that the God-man in his turn loves us with the love of his feeling human heart, of his spiritual human soul, and of his Divine nature. We respond by love of heart for heart. That's what Christmas is all about. Let's imitate St. Francis of Assisi. He originated the Christmas crib. If he couldn't be in Bethlehem at the birth of Jesus, he could at least put its images before his eyes. Like him, we should be found before the crib pouring out our love in return.

The family tree of Jesus helps us, too, to realize that God's love is stronger than sin. A woman who had been seriously tempted to commit suicide wrote a Christmas letter to a priest. She said she would not commit suicide; she would not give up on God's merciful love. She confided that in a notebook of sayings which help her, the most helpful one is, "There is no one whose sin is stronger than God's forgiving love."

Isn't that what this great feast is teaching us? Despite our whole history of sin, he came down. Anyone inclined to fear rather than love God should kneel at the crib, and ask, "Did God come to punish us? If so, it's a strange way to do it." Think of him there in Bethlehem, in need of the breast of his mother, and the hearts of us all. He still needs the hearts of us all, though he no longer needs to be nursed at the breast of his mother Mary. We help Mary to complete the work of the Incarnation by giving him ourselves in Holy Communion, for we too are his body. Who can ask a greater privilege, a greater love or a greater joy than that?

Then we will take our joy out into our daily lives, living like the body of Christ we are. Jesus is patient, so we'll be patient; Jesus is kind, so we'll be kind; Jesus is not jealous, so we won't be jealous; he's not puffed with pride, so we won't be, either; he's not rude, or self-seeking, or quick-tempered, or a nurser of grudges, so neither will we be. It sounds good; it sounds like we'll have a merry Christmas today and all year long!

"ABC" — Christmas Mass during the Day

Is 52:7-10
Heb 1:1-6
Jn 1:1-18

THE DAY OF OUR HAPPINESS

"The Word became flesh and dwelt among us." This is a day of great joy for us, and the more we understand and accept the mystery, the greater the joy. This feast — a birthday — is one we all understand, even the little children. And yet none of us understands this feast — the mystery of God become man.

Children delight in birthdays. When I was a little child, I used to enjoy going to the birthday parties of my friends, not to mention my own. Christmas is a birthday party. The birth happened two thousand years ago. The party is today.

We like to celebrate birthdays with light. We have lights on our birthday cakes, and lights on our Christmas trees. If we lit a light for each year since Jesus was born, what a blaze of light it would make! That reminds me of the old man who said, "No candles on my cake," and someone said, "Oh, why not?" And he said, "I can't blow out a forest fire!" Well, what if God lit a star for every year since he had his Son in eternity — or even for every century or millennium, or every eon? The thousands of billions of stars in the heavens wouldn't even make a beginning! See then what a mystery we are celebrating.

Think further about birthdays. On the Fourth of July, we celebrate the birth of a nation, but not as something that happened and stopped. The Fourth celebrates a birth and a birthday, because our nation lives on. So, too, we celebrate Jesus' birth and his birthday. He lives; he will live forever.

At this Mass we have the difficult Christmas Gospel. At midnight Mass, Jesus is born of Mary, and the angels tell the shepherds; at the dawn Mass, the shepherds arrive and worship. See from this that the Christmas Masses are really made for us to attend all three, for they progress through the mysteries. At this Mass we go far back, beyond the birth of Jesus in the Holy Family in time, to the origin or birth of Jesus in the Divine Family in eternity, from the Father, who had no beginning, who always was, and always had a Son, called the Word. And on Christmas, the Word was made flesh.

Stop on that one! What if one of your little kids came up to you and said, "Daddy (or Mommy), what does that mean, 'the Word was made flesh'?" Could you explain it? Can I? I think I can grasp it, though the mystery is beyond us in its fullness.

What does it mean? Well, we all know what a *word* is — or do we? We use plenty of them, but what they are is hard to explain. What is a word, really? Words have a spiritual beginning, in the mind. We speak of "conceiving" a thought, or "generating" ideas, as though they were our spiritual children. When we have a thought, we put it into a word — and sometimes we can't, can we? We struggle to find a word to convey it. Then, to communicate that word, we try to flesh it out, as it were, by sounding it with our lips, or by letters on paper. Do you see what we are finding? Basically, a word is something spiritual, which we embody in sounds or letters, to give it to our friends, and yet keep it ourselves.

Now, back to God's Word. When told that the Son of God is the Word of God, we are being told that God, who is a pure Spirit, fathered an image of himself, who is also a pure Spirit, and is everything that the Father is, except to be Father; and so he is God's Son. And when we hear that the Word was made flesh, we're being told that just as we embody an idea in a sound going forth from our lips, God sent his divine Son down into the world, and clothed him in flesh, to be seen by us.

At this Mass, we're reflecting on what it means that the Child born on Christmas is not just our Savior. He is Emmanuel, God-with-us, God become one of us, God clothed in flesh. But when we say "the Word became flesh," what does "flesh" mean? Does it mean that the Son of God took only a body like ours, and not a human mind and soul like ours? No, it uses the word *flesh* to mean our human nature, just as we say, "I'm glad to see you in the flesh," when we mean, "in person."

As a human being, Jesus is what we are. He is no Superman, no Six Million Dollar Man, no Super Brother to the Bionic Woman. He is a human being born of a woman. He lived a human life with joys and sorrows and pains and pleasures like our own. The Fathers of the Church drove home the fact of Jesus' full human nature by insisting that he redeemed only what he became, no more and no less. He is everything we are except sin; and he didn't redeem sin, he redeemed us from sin.

The Fathers of the Church said that Jesus is everything God is, and everything we are. Jesus is a true human being, born of a woman, while remaining true Son of God, born of God. He is the God-man. Jesus as God is the perfect image of the Father, and as Man he is God's image made flesh, the way we give our words a "body" of letters on paper or sounds in the air. His sweet presence in Bethlehem draws us up to love the God we cannot see. But Jesus doesn't just reveal God; he redeems man. St. Augustine says, "You would have suffered eternal death had he not been born in time."

What if your child asked, "What was the first Christmas present?" Would you say, "Jesus was the first Christmas present"? For the Bible says, "A Child is born to us, a Son is given to us." Born of our prayers, longings and needs, he is the beloved Son and Savior God gave as his gift to the human race. More, he is the Son of God become our Child, to make us children of God. That is what he became Man to accomplish.

When I finish, I can imagine someone saying, "Still, I wish I could go back to Bethlehem and hold him in my arms." I would, too, but Christianity doesn't go back; it goes forward to ever better things. And we can do something better. The shepherds could hold Jesus for just an instant; but the Child of Bethlehem has grown up, and we can take him into our hearts in Holy Communion. Is not that a far greater gift from him to us? Christmas is not just a birth recalled, but a birthday celebrated, the birthday of our living Lord and God. Let us receive him. Let us rejoice in him. Let us adore him.

"A" — Holy Family   Si 3:2-6, 12-14
Col 3:12-21
Mt 2:13-15, 19-23

HEALING THE FAMILY

The family needs healing in our day, and this Feast of the Holy Family is an eminent invitation to seek it.

The Bible speaks of family from its opening pages. God's word tells us that male and female together are God's image, but doesn't leave it at that. It exhorts man and woman to increase and multiply. This really changes the *image*. The human image of God it puts before us is *family!* And if we have any doubt of that interpretation, the Christian revelation should put it to rest. It tells us that the God of whom we are the image is a family. God is Three Persons.

The family has been honored through history. It is the dearest human companionship, the building block of society, the source of the future. It is God's own creation and God's image.

Yet the family is in trouble. Even apart from the troubles of any particular family, the family is in trouble simply by being in America. Forces are at work in our culture which make it a child-destroying and family-destroying culture.

Today's Gospel says "Herod is searching for the child to destroy him." Those words of 2,000 years ago apply today. Forces of evil have risen in our time to destroy both the child and its source.

The source of both child and family is sex and marriage. Both are under attack. Sex is made fruitless by contraception. Marriage is thrust aside to promote sex without children or commitment. Pregnancy is separated from birth by abortion. Since these evils are contagious, even good marriages are being infected and falling like leaves.

The evils go still further. Our society views the godlike gift of motherhood with contempt, as something to be manipulated and destroyed. This is no exaggeration. Some feminist circles scornfully describe pregnancy as the *curable venereal disease*. "Biology is not destiny" is their creed.

Abortion pioneeer Lawrence Lader writes, "Only when technology — and abortion is a crucial step in the process — allowed women to free themselves from the prison of incessant childbearing could they grapple with the possibility of achieving themselves on every plane." In this view, only when woman is mechanically and chemically manipulated to be other than herself is she free to be herself. Only when that in her which makes her most woman is destroyed, is she made equal to man.

Our society also subverts the child. It duns him with the notion that parental authority is obsolete and obedience out of date; that sex education is learning how to separate sex from marriage and life-giving.

Enough of the problems. What are the solutions? Can we begin by agreeing that God, who created man and woman, gives us sane solutions to all our problems?

The first help to healing the family is to put the use of sex back where God put it, in the way he put it there. He put it into married life, and into responsible use in marriage.

God's blueprint for family planning does not proceed by female manipulation or by killing preborn babies. It proceeds by informed self control. Today, informed self control means knowledge of the built-in natural family planning put into woman by nature and nature's God. It was used by primitive peoples in the past, and discovered by modern science in the present. Medical scientists have heeded the urging of recent popes that it be perfected and taught to married couples. When responsibly used, the Sympto-thermal method of natural family planning excels the reliability of some contraceptives, and is as moral as marriage. Most dioceses teach natural family planning.

The second help for healing the family is the restoration of holy and healthy relationships between the various family members. We all have to cultivate the virtues Christ singled out, in particular selfless love, forgiveness and thankfulness. A family with these virtues has at least the basic qualities for health and survival.

In the second reading, Paul describes certain norms for the Christian family. The man is appointed head of the family. Wives owe the final decision to husbands. This does not deny equality, or all of us are denied it. We all owe submission to one or another human authority. Furthermore, Paul exhorts all of us "to give in to one another's preferences out of reverence for Christ," who is head of us all. If a husband loves and respects his wife's needs and desires as Paul requires, he will be honoring her as much as she honors him by supporting his role as head of the family. One secular survey in fact reported that the happiest families were those in which the husband exercised a moderate leadership.

Two of the readings describe how children are to keep the fourth commandment, "Honor your father and your mother." Obedience, respect and gratitude are the virtues of good sons and daughters. Parents owe it to their children to cultivate these virtues in them from the first, even when the task is not pleasant. God's word praises such parents, and looks on disobedient children with horror. But everything is to be done in moderation. Paul cautions fathers not to badger their children lest they despair of pleasing. Above all, parents are to teach their children by word and example to love God above all and obey him in all.

How are we to escape the new Herod, the family-destroying forces in our culture? Perhaps the new "Egypt" in which to seek refuge is the voting booth. Some have used the fact that we live in a democracy as a chance to change society for the worse. We can use it to change society for the better.

As Christian families we need to remember that our greatest help is God. He has honored family life by living it. Pray for the help to imitate the Holy Family. By prayer and effort we can restore the family to holiness, health, and happiness.

"ABC" — Solemnity of Mary, Mother of God   Nb 6:22-27
and Giving the Name Jesus   Gal 4:4-7
Lk 2:16-21

MOTHER OF THE HIGHEST AND THE LOWEST

On this octave of Christmas we celebrate the maternity of Mary, the Mother of God, and rejoice in the day her divine Son was given his human name, Jesus. Let's begin by appreciating our Catholic privilege of knowing Mary so well.

A non-Catholic woman, Cornelia Otis Skinner, on visiting Rome, was inspired by the beautiful painting of the Sistine Madonna to write this poignant verse:

> Mary most serenely fair,
> Hear an unbeliever's prayer.
> Nurtured in an austere creed,
> Sweetest Lady, she has need
> Of the solace of thy grace.
> See the tears that stain her face,
> As she kneels to beg your love,
> You whom no one told her of.

This feast invites us to turn to Mary with a similar tender longing and love.

We can plunge into the untold depths of the drama of this feast by considering the three aspects of Mary's motherhood.

First, the mystery of Mary's motherhood is a great one. There is a great struggle and history and drama behind our rich Catholic doctrine about the maternity of Mary. We in the Catholic Church have clung to faith in the role of Mary through the ages. The Church in its early centuries labored to develop its theology of the mystery of Christ, and the role of the woman Scripture presents as his mother in the flesh.

By the fifth century, Mary had come to be called "Mother of God" — *Theotokos* in the Greek. But a bishop named Nestorius, offended by the title, demanded that it be dropped: How can a creature be the mother of the Creator? Great controversy followed, and the Church reflected as follows: It has been our faith from the beginning that Christ is the eternal Son of God. He was begotten of God before ever there was a creation. He was born again in time, in a human nature, of Mary the Virgin. Can this mother of his human nature rightly be called the Mother of God? That was the question to which Nestorius thundered *No!* For to call Mary *Theotokos* seems to be saying that God originated from Mary, a mere creature.

But other bishops answered that Christ Jesus is one undividable person with a human nature and a divine nature. And anyone who says Mary is the Mother of Jesus but not the Mother of God is dividing him into two persons. That is unacceptable. The same one person who was begotten of God in eternity was conceived in time in his human nature in the womb of Mary. The God-man is one person, so since Mary is the Mother of Jesus, you can call her the Mother of God.

To settle the issue, the world's bishops gathered in the Church of St. Mary at Ephesus in Asia Minor in an ecumenical council in the year 431. The faithful huddled in anguish and confusion at the doors, awaiting the decision: Was Jesus truly God or not? Was Mary *Theotokos* or not? On June 22 in the year 431, at twilight, the doors opened and a bishop began to read the decision: Mary is the Mother of God, Theotokos. Jesus is the Son of God . . . . The faithful interrupted with the cry, *Theotokos! Theotokos!*, and flooded the streets of Ephesus in candlelight procession proclaiming, "Mother of God! Mother of God!"

That is our faith. The decision safeguarded the mystery of Christmas, which is about nothing less than the eternal Son of God coming to human birth from Mary his human mother. When we call Mary the Mother of God, we obvious don't mean — and the

Catholic people know we don't mean — she is mother of the Godhead. No, she is mother of the humanity of the God who became man. That is the marvel and the mystery of our faith.

Not only is Jesus from Mary, he is like Mary. His human roots are in her flesh. He was brought up at her knee. In him is the likeness of Our Lady. St. Hippolytus says appealingly, "We know that his manhood was of the same clay as our own . . . If he were of a different substance from me, he would surely not have ordered me to do as he did . . . No. He wanted us to consider him as no different from ourselves, so he worked, he was hungry and thirsty, he slept. Without protest he endured his passion, he submitted to death and revealed the resurrection." There is the mystery of our faith, made so manifest by this feast of Mary's motherhood.

Some 1500 years after the birth of Christ, the Jesuit, St. Francis Xavier, wrote from India that "I have found that the people rebel at the Gospel every time I forget to show the image of Christ's mother next to the cross of the Savior." Isn't it marvelous that those oriental converts knew quite well how to distinguish Jesus from all the mythical incarnations of gods which their culture proposed? The incarnation of Christ is unique. It took place at a certain time on a certain day in a certain town in the womb of a certain woman whom history knows. These new converts understood that Mary serves Christ by her concreteness and her flesh and her motherhood, which pin down the fact that God became man. And so today we celebrate too the fact that the Son of God was given his human name, Jesus.

And now that other aspect of Mary's motherhood: Mary is Mother of the Church. Christ and his Church are united as vine and branch, head and members. As the divinity and humanity of Christ cannot be separated, neither can the person of Christ and his body the Church. And so the Second Vatican Council said, "We proclaim Mary to be the Mother of Christ and the Mother of the Church."

Finally, Mary is Mother of each of us: Each of us lives by the life of Mary's Child, so each of us is Mary's child. On the cross, Jesus said, "Behold your mother." Vatican Two taught that we are Mary's children in the order of grace. St. Augustine said that we come forth from the womb of Mary only when we enter eternal life.

The mystery we are celebrating began when God's angel told Mary God's plan, and she said, "Fiat," that is, "Be it done." One New Year's Eve a man remarked that at midnight the government and the scientists were adding one second to the length of the year. A companion said jokingly, "O good! We can accomplish much more this coming year." The first man asked, "What can you do in one second?" His companion replied, "You can say, 'Fiat!' " When we receive Jesus in the Eucharist today, let us take one second to say our "Fiat," and invite Jesus to continue in us the work begun on the day Mary became Mother of God.

"ABC" — Epiphany

Is 60:1-6
Ep 3:2-3, 5-6
Mt 2:1-12

CHRISTIAN FAITH FOR THE WORLD

What happened to the three wise men that first Epiphany day is repeated each day through history. Prepared for us today by the Lord and his Church is the grace of rediscovering Christ anew in this hour. What each one of us should ask ourselves is this: Do I really feel I have found Christ as those wise men did? They were certain they had found him. They offered him gifts of great value, gifts symbolic of worship: gold, frankincense and myrrh. Has my faith enabled me to find Christ with that kind of conviction? If not, why not? If not, I'd better take my faith and shake it, as we do a watch that doesn't go.

So I'd like to reflect on faith with you, and if I hear you

shaking your faith, I'll say, "Good!" One priest, offering Mass in a temporary auditorium was blinded by the stage lights and said to the congregation: "The lights are so bright I'm making an act of faith — I hope somebody is out there!" That's the way our faith is. God sees us, but we don't see him — but we will. We live in expectation.

For our reflection on faith, I'll pose three questions: What is faith? Why do we believe? And how do we find Christ by faith?

First, what is faith? My first answer is a true story. On a fishing trip, a father sent his little boy up on the dock while he launched the boat, maneuvered it close, and called, "Son, you can't see me, but I can see you. Jump, and you'll land in my arms." Hearing the lapping waters and the voice out of the darkness, the boy was frightened. Bravely, he jumped — and landed in his father's arms. That's faith — trusting dialogue between us and our heavenly Father. "You can't see me," the Father is saying to us, "but do what I tell you and you are going to end up in my arms." Faith is as simple as that. It's our communication with God.

For the wise men, faith came from the Jewish Scriptures, where they read of the promised Messiah, and the star that Micah the prophet said would rise out of Jacob. The star rose, and they believed, and set out on their journey. Notice that: Faith was more than an inner assent. It was their lives on the line. There is more than meets the eye here. Tell me something, and I either believe or not. But when God reveals to us — that is, tells us something — he helps us to say yes. He works in our hearts and minds. St. Paul says, "The Holy Spirit gives witness to our spirit that we are the children of God."

The wise men followed the star, reached Bethlehem, saw a mother, and with her a new-born child. They had found the Messiah, the Savior of the world. The star that rises in our lives is Christ, our Light.

In that first reading, the prophet prophesies there will be a great light for Jerusalem. Christ is that light of Jerusalem and the world. Faith is our response. Faith can be expressed in many ways. It is an assent to the wisdom of God, who tells us the way to live, the way to go, and the way to reach eternal life. Faith is assent to the light that leads us to love. That Babe of Bethlehem is the love of God made flesh, for God is love. By following the way of faith, we are following the light of love.

At our baptism came the question: "What do you ask of the Church of God?" Answer: "The faith." Question: "What does the faith bring you?" Answer: "Eternal life." Faith is the response to God that leads us to his eternal life. Faith is like walking. When you walk, one foot is always reaching out. Faith is a foot put into the future, toward God. Faith is a journey into eternity, symbolized by the wise men's journey to Bethlehem.

There are always obstacles to faith. The families and friends of the wise men must have thought that they were setting out on a fool's journey. They surely put obstacles in their way. Our world places obstacles in our way. It's upset by many teachings of the Church. The word of God forbids many things the world is set on doing, so if we live the faith, we're the enemy of the world.

Secondly, then: Why do we believe? We believe on the evidence. Our first reading and Psalm foretold that peoples from all over the world would come to Jerusalem to worship the true God. Today, over a billion Christians have made the journey to Jerusalem in fact or in spirit. So our faith is based on evidence. Think of the miracles at Lourdes, the miracles throughout history, the moral miracle of holiness in the Church despite all the tearing at faith and morals. Every time we hear the Gospel of holiness preached, despite the battles to silence it, we are witnessing an aspect of that moral miracle. One could speak for hours on the reasons and proofs for the faith we hold.

Finally, then: How do we find Christ by faith? By being strong. Didn't that little boy have to be strong to believe his father, to believe words, words, words? To trust his father, he had to have enough guts, character and personality to put his belief into practice. Often, faith gets stuck at the first stage. People believe, and do nothing. We can find Christ by being strong. What is faith but strength of will, strength of character, strength of love to say yes to God when he tells us what he is and what we are to do?

Don't you think that's true? I do. I've been trying to communicate to you these last few minutes what faith has meant to me, and I have given my life to it. And this is the meaning faith has come to have for me — I have to say by my life, "God, I believe," as the wise men did. In the postcommunion prayer, we ask God, "Guide us with your light. Help us to recognize Christ in this Eucharist and welcome him with love." Our meeting with Jesus is more wonderful than the one the wise men enjoyed. In the Eucharistic mystery, Jesus communicates himself to us completely.

One closing thought: The wise men had to go into Bethlehem and ask, "Do you know of a woman who recently became the mother of a little son?" By inquiring about Mary, they found Christ the Messiah. When struggling with faith, go to Mary, so tender and loving. Go to Mary, for wherever Mary is, you will find Jesus there.

"A" — Baptism of the Lord   Is 42:1-4, 6-7
                                          Ac 10:34-38
                                          Mt 3:13-17

THIS MYSTERIOUS BAPTISM

When the whole board of directors of a great company assemble, the employees are set all abuzz. What is going on? Are major decisions being made? How will it affect their status and their lives? In today's Gospel, a far more momentous event is taking

place. For the first time in recorded history, the three Persons of the
Blessed Trinity together are disclosing themselves to the world. In a
voice from heaven, the Father is heard; in the form of a dove, the Holy
Spirit is manifested; and by the voice and the dove the young man
being baptized in the Jordan is revealed as the Incarnate Son of God.

Why this great theophany, this unmatched divine self-revela-
tion? What is transpiring that will affect our status and our lives? The
answer is that the most Blessed Trinity is revealing the Son of God as
our Savior, and calling us to the baptism he is instituting.

Isn't it striking that some Christian parents neglect their
children's baptism when Jesus Christ did not neglect his, and in
fact insisted on it against John the Baptizer's objections? Jesus'
baptism was so important that all four Gospels focus on it.

Why was Jesus baptized? What is he calling us to do? How are
we to do it?

Why was Jesus baptized? Certainly, not because he was a
sinner. Scripture tells us he was like us in all things except sin.
Then why was he baptized? St. Paul gives us the terrible answer.
He was "made sin" for us. So identified with us was he when he
made us his body that our sins were accounted his sins.

He went down into the waters, not to wash his body born of
Mary, but to wash his mystical body which we would become by
baptism. He sanctified the world's waters to begin the new creation
by water and the Holy Spirit. Through signs and wonders at the
Jordan, the Holy Trinity celebrated the gift of baptism they were
giving the world.

As Moses entered the waters of the Red Sea to lead the people
to the promised land of Israel, Jesus enters the waters of Israel to
lead us to the promised land of heaven.

What is the Blessed Trinity calling us to do? The Father calls
us to believe in his divine Son, the Son calls us to baptism, and the
Holy Spirit calls us to repentance of sin, holiness, and a life like to
Christ's own.

By baptism we confessed our sins, and were reborn the

children of God. But the great battle against sin in our lives was just beginning. From then on we had the role of imitating Christ, who is so beautifully depicted in our first reading from Isaiah. He is so tender, he never breaks even a bruised reed, and so gentle that he never puts out a spark of hope as small as that in a smoking wick. Surely, in Isaiah's prophecy we recognize the Heart of Jesus Christ. He is the tireless Servant of God, sent to free all peoples from the dungeons of death by giving them rebirth as God's children.

In Isaiah's Suffering Servant do we recognize not only Christ but also ourselves? Our struggle to imitate Christ and grow into our new identity as children of God must go on. Christ was willing to be taken for a sinner because in us his mystical body there is sin. Will we deny our sins or confess them and take up the struggle against them?

It is interesting that even some psychiatrists tell us how harmful it is to deny our failings, weaknesses and limitations. Carl Jung writes that it seems to be a sin in nature to hide our insufficiency. Karen Horney says that the root of neurotic sickness is the compulsion to deny all the negatives in us, and waste our energies trying to support a deluded vision of a self that never was and never will be.

The faithful of Christ see their imperfections and confess them, but also labor against them, knowing that by effort and grace and forgiveness of sin they will be changed into radiant likenesses of the Son of God. That is no neurotic dream. It is being faithful to our baptismal calling, as we pleaded to be in the opening prayer.

That is our calling, but what are we to do to live it and carry it out? Not surprisingly, we were given the answer at our baptism. We were informed that when we went down into the water, it was to be buried with Christ, and when we came up with the blessing of the Holy Trinity, we rose with Christ into newness of life. And so we were asked if we renounced Satan and all his works and empty promises, and the answer was, "I do."

Then we were anointed with the holy oil of salvation, and told that we were to live as a member of the body of the Christ who was anointed Priest, Prophet, and King. That is, we inherited a share in Christ's priesthood, and his role of spreading the Gospel, and his power to govern creation.

If you imagine this is an empty symbolic statement, stop, look and listen. In your mind's eye, gaze round the world at the work being done to spread Christ's kingdom. Who is offering his Sacrifice, spreading his Gospel, and laboring to bring the world under God's dominion? Is it anybody but us, the members of his body by baptism? When we fail to do his work, the work fails to be done.

If the Jewish people recognized themselves in the Servant of God whom Isaiah described, how much more should we, who are members of the Christ Isaiah was foretelling?

Today the most Holy Trinity, the divine Board of Directors of creation, are pointing to Christ as our way, our truth and our life. Our life in him began at baptism. It continues as, like him, we go about doing good works and bringing healing to all who are in the grip of the devil. We don't have to be Superman to do it. Whether we are single or married, religious or priests, we only have to use the graces of baptism to sanctify all the activities of our state of life.

Today when you receive the body of Christ, say, "Lord, I who receive your sacred body am a member of your body. Help me to show it in thought, word and deed."

"A" — Second Sunday of the Year   Is 49:3, 5-6
                                                   1 Cor 1:1-3
                                                   Jn 1:29-34

JESUS' BAPTISM AND OURS

"This is God's chosen one." This declaration of John the Baptist brings a striking force to bear upon us. If we believe Christ is the Chosen One, we are compelled to believe more widely and broadly in our own call. Having recognized Christ, we must come to recognize who we are in Christ.

If Christ is the Chosen One who was sent, as Isaiah prophesied, to be "a light to the nations," then we are the ones he came to call. Called to what? The Church tells us clearly: called to be God's children and servants in Christ, and made so by our baptism.

In a sense, the Incarnation which we celebrated on Christmas advances a step in each of us. In this liturgy, we are doing more than recalling the mystery of Christ; we are experiencing that mystery moving forward in history and coming to fullness as Christ continues to incarnate himself in us, his new members.

Last week, we celebrated the Baptism of Christ. This week, we hear the Baptizer recall how he recognized Jesus as the Chosen One only when he baptized him. Do we recognize who we are by our baptism? We need to reflect on ourselves, to probe our identity. The Church, having baptized us, recognizes us as the body of Christ. What are the consequences of that recognition?

Well, as Christ is, so is his body. We recognize Christ in that prophecy of Isaiah about the Suffering Servant of God. We recognize Christ in the Psalm which says, "Here am I, Lord. I come to do your will." The question is, do we also recognize ourselves there? For we cannot live as his body without serving and suffering with him, any more than we can rise from the dead in him without sharing his glory.

Christ said, "I have come that they may have life and have it more abundantly." Have you ever said to yourself, "As a member of Christ, I have been sent that people may have life, and have it more abundantly"? We share Christ's role.

Our role in promoting life calls us to take a responsible stand for life in our country. Each year, in January, we recall with grief the immoral Supreme Court decision of 1973, Roe vs. Wade, which stripped preborn children of their right to life. That decision is contrary to the Declaration of Independence in which our founding fathers justified the birth of this nation. They wrote that "We hold these truths to be self-evident, that all men are created equal, that they are endowed by their Creator with certain unalienable rights, that among these are life, liberty and the pursuit of happiness." The Supreme Court of 1973 trampled the God-given rights of babies, and trampled upon the very reasons for writing any law. As Supreme Court justice Sandra Day O'Connor has said, the law "is now on a collision course with itself." It is also in collision with God and all who recognize and respect God's law.

Let no one deceive you with false arguments about when life begins. The medical journal, *California Medicine*, which favors the abortion decision, wrote that we have adopted new moral norms which permit abortion, but don't like to call it killing. The journal adds, "The result has been a curious avoidance of the scientific fact, which everybody really knows, that human life begins at conception and is continuous whether intra- or extra-uterine, until death." Can anyone say more clearly that abortion is murder?

If pregnant women were transparent, so you could see the children in their wombs, would anyone any longer dare to support abortion? Since they are not transparent, we must use our minds to teach our hearts. "Do unto others," Jesus said, "as you would have others do unto you."

Roe vs. Wade has brought us our own Holocaust. By 1988, some twenty million legal abortions had been performed since Roe vs. Wade. More children are slaughtered every two years by abortions than in all of our American wars together.

Abortion is a one-sided war between parents and their own children. It is also a war against God, the Author of Life. There are no winners. Parents are victims along with the children they have aborted. Consciences are slaughtered. Eternal life is slaughtered. Most of those slaughtered children have been deprived of the opportunity for baptism.

Today, women who have had abortions describe how they have been victimized by their culture, and sometimes by their own families and husbands and other lovers. They feel they have been deceived and manipulated and brainwashed into betraying not only their child, but themselves and their God. An organization named Women Exploited By Abortions has been founded by these victim women. It seeks to awaken other women and other parents to the horror of abortion before they too fall victim.

We are children of God, we are members of Christ. It is our role to see that all have life, and have it more abundantly. One man said to a priest, "I think that people sit around waiting for someone in a white chariot to come and solve their problems." We are the solution to our problems. We are the hands of Christ.

Go in spirit to the Blessed Mother who holds her Christ Child close. Ask what she thinks of abortion. Ask what you should do about it, then listen and feel her answer within your heart.

With the help of God's grace, we are the solution to our problems and those of the world. Our baptism has made us a new creation. We are the body of Christ. We are the hands of Jesus. Are we using them to renew the world?

"A" — Third Sunday of the Year   Is 8:23-9:3
                                                  1 Cor 1:10-13
                                                  Mt 4:12-23

THE MEANING OF LIFE

The earth is one vast magnet. The little metal sliver of the compass needle is drawn by it. So is the human heart drawn by its goods and pleasures. But bring a more powerful magnet near the compass of the human heart, and it is swept into captivity. And so when Christ came near, the young fishermen "immediately abandoned their nets and became his followers."

So the Gospel records. Having heard the three readings, what do you think God's message is for us today? A priest asks himself that question each time he prepares a homily. He searches for the meaning until the three readings fall into a pattern and point like an arrow toward what God and his Church are saying to us. In the Office of the Church this week is the phrase, "Come let us praise the Lord; in Him is all our delight." Those words are the pith of what today's readings are telling us.

The light of Christ, light of love, has come into the world as Isaiah foretold. The Son of God walked this earth, and a great light shone out. It is the light that led the first disciples to leave all and follow him. We live in that light, that love, that meaning.

Don't we all experience that love when deepest into prayer and our relationship with Christ? Don't we see his light in our minds and feel his love in our hearts? Is there anyone here who can honestly deny having the experience? If so, pray for it! It pleases God to give that gift. Christ came to give it. Christ's message is deeper than words. It seeps into our hearts at the very roots of our being and we sense in him the very meaning of our existence. We feel nourished like a plant fed at its roots. In that sustenance we taste the very meaning of our lives.

One Jewish writer spoke of his experience in a German death camp. In that very deprivation, almost beyond endurance, he discovered that the meaning of life is love. Why be surprised? God is love. All other loves are like tributaries from the infinity of the sea of God's love. Christ, the light of the world, the love of the world, wakens and stirs love in us. Habakkuk, the prophet, expressed the depth of the love he had found in God when he wrote, "For though the fig tree blossom not, nor fruit be on the vines, though the yield of the olive fail and the terraces produce no nourishment, though the flocks disappear from the stalls, yet will I rejoice in the Lord and exult in my saving God."

To waken love, the lover tells the beloved what he has done for her, and stands ready to do. Paul does that. He talks of stonings, scourgings, shipwrecks, persecutions, labors, all for love of God and his people. The things Paul has lost he looks on as less than nothing because God has conquered his heart. That is the depth of love we are being called to today. When the love of God really comes into our lives, it sweeps all else away. A spider's web can no more hold a great ship in a raging gale than earth's things can hold the human heart when God's love storms in.

This past week we celebrated the feast of St. Agnes, the twelve-year-old girl martyr. She was threatened with torture if she clung to Christ, and promised a fine bridegroom and rich gifts if she renounced him. It was like empty wind in her ears. Wanting only her Divine Bridegroom, she went blissfully to martyrdom. Are we slow learners? Where are we when the love of God comes storming into human lives?

We should sense this divine love storming into the lives of the young fishermen in today's Gospel. Christ comes and sweeps them away on his torrent.

In a novel entitled *Melvin Goodwin, USA,* by John Marquand, one of the characters, Dottie Peale, is flying over the Atlantic during the Second World War in the dead of night. Fearing imminent death, she probes her life, and says to her companion, "Sid, I wonder what everything's been about." The apostles found out in time. St. Agnes the martyr found out by twelve. God willing, we have all found out, or will find out, and be swept along on that torrent of God's love, and discover the secrets and the joy and the glory of it as did the disciples and Agnes and all the saints.

In the second reading Paul laments over those who have not experienced Christ this way. Some are so far from this experience that they don't know Christ from Peter or Apollos or Paul. Paul cannot tolerate such nonsense. Peter and Apollos and Paul and the theologians and the preachers are mere communicators of and fellow-sharers in the mystery of Christ. If we are wise, we follow no theologian, no priest, no pope. We follow Christ. We obey the Pope because he has been appointed to teach the word of Christ.

But we follow Christ, Christ our love, Christ our light, Christ our God. Paul makes the same point plainly when he asks, "Were you baptized into me? Was I crucified for you?" And he might have added, "And if I was, what good would it have done?"

We were baptized into Christ, plunged into his life, and in the Eucharist plunged into his love. Christ said, "I have come to light a fire on the earth and I cannot wait till it is accomplished." He is setting his fire of love. Don't we sense that is what we truly want? But, O, how we cling to our little shreds of present happiness and fear it will be lost. It will indeed be lost, lost in the torrent of his gift of happiness and joy. Hence the Psalmist writes, "How precious is your steadfast love, O God! The children of men take refuge in the shadow of your wings. They feast on the abundance of your house, and you give them drink from the river of your delights. For with you is the fountain of life; in your light do we see light."

When God's love storms into lives, it produces priests and brothers and sisters and lay apostles and saintly people of every kind. In this life may we all be swept along together in the onrush of God's love, and in eternity drink forever at the torrent of his pleasure. "For eye has not seen, nor ear heard, nor has it entered into the mind of man to imagine the things that he has prepared for those who love him."

"A" — Fourth Sunday of the Year

Zp 2:3; 3:12-13
1 Cor 1:26-31
Mt 5:1-12

MORAL LIVING ON A NEW PLATEAU

A visitor to Boston, introduced to a stuffed shirt, tried to win him over by what he thought was praise. "These Bostonian elite," he said, "are not the snobs I heard they were. The ones I met met me half way." "Obviously," the stuffed shirt sniffed, "you haven't met the right people."

We can laugh because pride and pretension are absurd. If you have any doubts, stand at a few more births and attend a few more burials. Learn that we have nothing we have not received, and can keep nothing we have gathered.

The readings today are about attitudes, and they are either stifling or liberating depending on our own attitude. How clear they make it that God can't endure the smell of pride even in the great, and still less in the mediocre.

Why? Fundamentally, because humility is the truth, and pride a lie, and God hates lies. But also — and perhaps this is even more fundamental — because the proud aren't free to love. They're so busy measuring the worth of others with their false tape measures that they're inaccessible to natural friendships and impervious to falling in love.

Contrast that with the Christian attitude, found in the opening prayer. We beg God to help us love all as he loves them. If God, like the proud, restricted friendships to those who measure up to what he has and is, who could be his friends?

But Jesus carries the matter much further by exalting the poor in spirit, the sorrowing, and the hungry for holiness to the plateau of blessedness. How can that be when the world thinks that the wealthy who need nothing are the lucky ones?

The answer is that there is no mortal who needs nothing. We all have needs, and these people are blessed because they have blessed needs. They are free of materialism, free to live the Christian moral life, which is founded on selfless love.

Don't think the Christian moral life can be fulfilled by living the ten commandments. They are only the foundation on which we build a life of virtue. They mostly tell us what not to do and what not to be. The beatitudes, on the other hand, tell us what to do and what to become. They counsel attitudes and actions which are the flowering of every virtue. The proud, of course, consider the beatitudes unreal or even ridiculous.

The beatitudes teach us that just when we think we have lost everything, we have gained blessedness. The poor man who is poor and doesn't mind because he trusts in God's care is blessed. The rich man who finds that God has become so dear to him that his wealth means nothing is truly blessed. The person who sorrows over the evil-doing all around him is not lessened by his loss of worldly joy; he is blessed by his share in Christ's own sorrow. The people who so hunger and thirst for God that they have lost their pleasure in the things of this world are not deprived; they are enriched by the first taste of the companionship of God. The people who are so merciful they look like soft-hearted fools to the proud are blessed because they will have all the mercy they will ever need to assure their eternal salvation.

And now a serious question: Why do so few seem to under-stand the beatitudes, or hold the opinion that they can be practiced only by the saints, when in fact Jesus addressed them to us all? I think the theologians give us a thought-provoking answer. They tell us that as long as we govern our lives by our own common sense we can neither understand nor practice the beatitudes. That is because the beatitudes go beyond common sense to God's sense of things. They can be practiced only by those who are attuned to the Holy Spirit and make use of his gifts.

Let me give examples of the connection between the beatitudes and the gifts of the Holy Spirit. We can be "poor in spirit" only if we use the Spirit's gift of Fear of the Lord. It is not a cringing fear, but a loving fear of offending our divine Father. It makes our desire to please God grow and grow, so that the earthly things that stand in the way of our desire mean less and less, until finally we have that freedom from their hold on us that is poorness in spirit. We can be lowly only if we use the Spirit's gift of piety. It makes us really know God as a loving Father, and all others as God's children, and therefore our equals as brothers and sisters in Christ.

Since Jesus did address the beatitudes to us all, why do so few let the Holy Spirit guide them? Perhaps the chief reason is that many people have far more desire to make progress in the world than in their love of God. They don't want to be poor in spirit, because they don't wish to desire less of all the passing things of this world. They have no interest in how much they can do for God, but only in how little they can do and still be saved. They spend all their lives along the borders of the ten commandments, and no one really knows how many fall off those borders and drown in the sea of sin forever.

Then there are others who want to ascend to the land of the beatitudes, and they ask the way. They are told that each one has to listen to the Spirit within, for no one else can guide them. But to hear the Spirit reliably, they must avoid all deliberate sin, even venial; and they must pray often, to develop what is called the interior life, for it is within the heart that the Spirit draws us on. Many decide that they are too busy with life now, but later on they'll find time. Little do they realize that if even in their youthful ardor they don't make the necessary sacrifices to follow Christ the whole way, it would take a miracle to do it when age cools their ardor and consumes their energies.

Finally, there are those who really love the Lord, and nothing is too much to ask. Off they go on their journey to the beatitudes, that is, to the way of life that Jesus lived. Happy are they, for the kingdom of God is theirs.

"A" — Fifth Sunday of the Year

Is 58:7-10
1 Cor 2:1-5
Mt 5:13-16

THE MORALITY THAT ATTRACTS

St. John Vianney, a parish priest, was so known for his wisdom and mercy in the confessional that he attracted penitents from far and wide. Saints like him should draw us all to Christ, for "If this is the servant, how wonderful must be the Master!"

That is rather obvious, is it not? But now for the surprise. The Master expects all of us to inspire that same reaction in people who come to know us. "Your light must shine before men," he declares, "so that they may see goodness in your acts and give praise to your heavenly Father."

Some people practice a cold, calculating morality that repels others. The Lord is making it clear that our moral tone must be different; it must not have that effect.

Today's Gospel reading is instructing us in this matter. The reading is a continuation of Jesus' Sermon on the Mount. From that Sermon, the beatitudes were given us last week. Now Jesus is describing the effects of the beatitudes. They can make us shine with an appealing holiness that gives light to the world; and the peace they produce in us can help us treat with others in a way that will encourage and preserve goodness in them the way salt preserves food.

What is the beatitude that most makes our light shine out to people, and helps to preserve peace? There is good reason to think it is the fourth beatitude: "Blessed are the merciful, for they shall obtain mercy." Mercy is the noblest expression of love, and is characteristic of God himself. The Psalms tell us that God's mercy is over all his works.

To help us grasp the true nature of mercy, let us compare it with pity and compassion. Pity is sympathetic sorrow for one suffering. Compassion is pity plus the will to help. Mercy is pity plus the will to help, plus the helping. The Good Samaritan of Jesus' famous parable showed pity, compassion, and the mercy that saved the helpless man's life.

When Christ came to our help, he went beyond ordinary compassion, and in the beatitudes he and the Holy Spirit are teaching us to do the same. In an ordinary act of compassion, we come along as a kind of savior that makes the helped person feel both inferior to us and indebted to us. But God's compassion came to us out of a higher wisdom that eliminates this sense of inferiority in the helped one. St. Paul describes this wisdom in the second reading. That wisdom is Christ crucified.

Christ the Son of God went to such extremes to help us that he ended up in need of the pity, the compassion and the mercy of all he came to help. When we see him hanging on the cross, we know that he needs the mercy of our gift of love, and the gift of our acceptance of his salvation. Otherwise, we leave him the most despised of men. Furthermore, by becoming man he became loving Brother of us all, and so he suffers when any of us suffers. Do you realize what that means? It means that when we relieve the suffering of even one of his sisters or brothers, we relieve his suffering. That is why he said, "What you do to the least of these, my brethren, you do to me."

None of this is any exaggeration. Pope John Paul II, in his encyclical, *Rich in Mercy,* says that to offer our Savior love "is not only an act of solidarity with the suffering Son of Man, but also a kind of 'mercy' shown by each one of us to the Son of the eternal Father."

This mystery of Christ's mercy, which is so lowly that he needs from us the mercy of accepting it, is at the heart of all the beatitudes and the whole Christian life. St. Paul manifests that Christlike mercy. He describes to the Corinthians how he came bringing salvation, but came weak and fearful and in need of mercy himself.

The prophets of old already preached mercy, as we heard in the reading of Isaiah. But when Christ preached it, he went beyond their teaching to a way of giving that created the need for a reverse mercy as well. Thus did he preserve the worth and dignity of all. He came to save a wounded race, and ended a healer who was wounded and in need of the healing balm of our love returned. If we follow him well, we experience this too. At times at least, we should so impoverish ourselves in serving others that we need the mercy of the ones we serve. Isn't that the secret of the poor and simple Francis of Assisi, who still wins the heart of much of the world?

Doesn't this mystery of reverse compassion also explain the true meaning of devotion to the Sacred Heart of Jesus? Jesus asks us to heal his Heart by turning from the coldness of sin, and doing penance for the salvation of ourselves and others. If you look closely, you'll see how selfless his plea is. He is really saying, "Make me happy by making yourself and others happy with the Father forever."

Mary is the model of the merciful follower of Jesus. We know instinctively that we are part of her happiness, so that for her to refuse us would be to refuse herself. And so we pray with confidence, "Remember, O most gracious Virgin Mary, that never was it known that anyone who fled to thy protection, implored thy help or sought thy intercession was left unaided."

Our morality, inspired by the beatitudes, is a morality that attracts because it is a morality that serves in the lowly spirit of Christ. May our Father in heaven make us the good Samaritans, the salt of the earth, and the light of the world, reflecting the radiant love of the heart of Mary and the Heart of the Son of God.

"A" — Sixth Sunday of the Year   Si 15:15-20
                                                              1 Cor 2:6-10
                                                              Mt 5:17-37

THE HIGHER LAW OF CHRIST

An old man with a terrible leg condition said to a priest, "It's my own fault. Five or six years ago, the doctor warned me, and told me what to do, but I didn't do it." Today, it is the divine Physician who tells us what to do. Will we do it?

In the Gospel, Christ pronounces a fierce condemnation of

divorce and remarriage. Who can survey the marriage carnage around us and not see the cost of failing to obey? Even so, to fully understand the passionate feelings of Christ we need to turn from the wounded state of marriage to its glory in the beginning. Those fortunate enough to attend daily Mass last week heard God's word describing how God created the world, created man, and then created woman his equal partner, thus creating marriage.

How conceive the beauty of that moment? The first man stood with the first woman in the garden of God's presence. It is the original love story. Only in the light of its glory can we grasp Christ's passionate reestablishment of the permanence of the marriage vow.

Pope John Paul II, in a whole series of talks, meditated on this original unity of man and woman. He asks us to reflect on its unrepeatable beauty. He speaks of the depth and force of this first and original emotion of the man, the masculine presence, with the feminine presence before him. Who can describe the mood, the feelings, the love stirring in their hearts as they beheld their fulfillment in one another, stood in naked innocence before one another, and saw in one another their complementarity and fullness? In their hearts was an innocent love overbrimmed with joy, and an innocent joy overbrimmed with love. It was an unrepeatable moment. Yet, to a degree, it is repeated every time a boy and girl meet and fall in love and marry. Only in this light does the word of Christ rush upon us in its full force, and his fierceness against sin become understandable.

Christ, the new Moses, renewed marriage and social living. He came to restore what was lost when Adam and Eve sinned and what was lost wherever there was sin. But to grasp to the full Christ's passionate purpose, we have to be aware he was responding to the charge that he was destroying Jewish laws and customs. To his detractors he responds that in truth he is advancing the law to its fulfillment.

Christ freed us from such lesser laws as washing hands and

cups to free our energies to live to the full the law of innocent love. It is our *hearts* we must purify; our energies must pour into remaining faithful to love in marriage and all human relationships. As murder is wrong, so are the anger, hostility and unforgiveness which kill love. As adultery and premarital sex are wrong, so are the impure thoughts which lead to them.

Remarriage after divorce is forbidden because the glory of that moment when husband and wife become one body must not be destroyed. Christ's grace makes perseverance possible.

To maintain marital holiness and joy, spouses must love God above all things and obey his laws of creation and re-creation in Christ. Only by reverence for God's law can they love one another with the selfless intensity he intended. Just as manufacturers of cars tell you how you must care for your car if you don't want it to break down, the Creator of marriage charges spouses with the laws that preserve love and fidelity and eternal salvation.

Put more profoundly, the God-man is our law. We walk in his likeness. St. John writes, "The way we can be sure we are in union with him is for the man who claims to abide in him to conduct himself just as he did." A shorthand rule for guiding our conduct is to ask, "Would Christ do it if he were in my shoes? Then I will do it. Would Christ refuse? Then I will refuse."

Finally, we can be molded into Christ only by the wisdom of the Church of Christ and the Spirit of Christ. St. Paul speaks of this wisdom in the second reading. The Church and the Holy Spirit speak with one voice because the Spirit guides the Church.

The Holy Spirit guides us where the Church is silent. Church and Scripture teach us both of the holiness of marriage, and of the privilege of sacrificing it to follow Christ, but only the Holy Spirit can tell you to which you are called.

Can the Holy Spirit ever contradict the teaching of the Scriptures and the Church? He is the source of both! To know this and practice it is the wisdom of the spiritually mature of which Paul speaks in the second reading.

At times, spouses are so overwhelmed by marriage problems and so taken captive by the world's false solutions, that the law of God seems unreal. When marriage becomes a battleground, what are they to do? There is a certain parallel between marital wars, and wars between states. So listen to what General Douglas MacArthur, a man of the world, sometimes called the greatest general of our time, said to the American people on the question of war and peace:

"The problem basically is theological, and involves a spiritual . . . improvement of human character that will synchronise with our almost matchless advances in science, art, literature and all material and cultural developments . . . It must be of the spirit if we are to save the flesh."

Must not the flesh that has become one by marriage all the more be saved by the spirit? Isn't marital peace available from the Spirit of Christ to all who really want it, and work and pray for it?

To be faithful to one another, spouses must remember their higher calling. We Christians are molded by the Holy Spirit into Christ's likeness, and are drawn with Christ to a destiny beyond even the best things of this life. "Eye has not seen," Paul writes, "nor ear heard, nor has it dawned on man to imagine what God has prepared for those who love him."

Will we reach our destiny? The first reading tells us we can. "Before man are set life and death; whichever he chooses will be given him." May we all choose life in Christ. May married couples entrust their union to him, and find the joy he intended for them.

"A" — Seventh Sunday of the Year   Lv 19:1-2, 17-18
                                                     1 Cor 3:16-23
                                                     Mt 5:38-48

MESSIANIC LICENSE

A wise man has said that genius is the ability to see relationships, and so learn how alike one another seemingly different things really are. Einstein exemplified that genius when he discovered that matter and energy are simply two forms of the same reality. One can be transformed into the other, as a nuclear energy plant now makes evident.

When Christ came bearing God's wisdom, he revealed new relationships of love more startling than nuclear reactions. Certainly, if matter and energy are mysterious, love is a greater and less understood mystery, and only the Son of God and his saints reveal it to us in all its splendor and its many surprises.

In today's readings we have a perspective on God's gradual revelation of love as the basis of the ten commandments and of all moral living. In the first reading, we heard what God revealed about love through Moses. He taught that we must be holy because he is holy, and he made it evident that we can be holy only if we love as he loves. Thus God himself is our first love and our motive for all love, and our love is to be fashioned in the likeness of his love. Love excludes hatred, grudges, and revenge. "You shall love your neighbor," God commands, "as yourself."

That command of love of neighbor should have hung bright as the sun in the sky of humanity's moral life, but it was in fact obscured by the clouds of false interpretation until Jesus made it shine undimmed. For various people had their own ideas of who their neighbor was, and restricted their love accordingly. But Jesus dispersed the clouds and rejected the restrictions. "Who is your neighbor?" he asked, and implied the answer in the parable of the good Samaritan. Now we know that our neighbor is everyone.

Love, like the light of the sun, is to go out to all. All are children of the same heavenly Father, and we are to exclude none from our love.

At this point, Jesus' listeners may have felt their love being stretched like a rubber band, and wondered when it would break. But the best — or the worst — was yet to come.

"Love your enemies, pray for your persecutors," Jesus *taught*. That command was too much for some. By it, the worldly-wise are outraged, even among Christians. That is why Paul tells us in the second reading that if we are wise in worldly ways, we'd better become fools, "for the wisdom of this world is absurdity to God."

Actually, a little reflection can show that what the world considers wise is often stupid. Think of a man returning from a hunting trip, gun in hand. He sees a man striking his brother, and feels a raging impulse to shoot him dead — and in the nick of time sees that the attacker is his other brother!

The teaching of Christ is that the other man is *always* our brother. We are all children of a single Father. Once that registers, love of our enemies makes eminent sense. We hate the evil they do, but never the doers.

Abraham Lincoln once released a Southern soldier from prison to work on his needy mother's farm. A northern woman, hearing of this, stormed at the President: "You don't free your enemies, you destroy them!" Lincoln replied, "Madam, if I make my enemy my friend, don't I destroy my enemy?" Isn't that exactly what Jesus intends when he commands, "Love your enemy"?

This refusal to fight violence with violence and hatred with hatred has been called MESSIANIC LICENSE. Recall that a license is a permission from legitimate authority to act in a certain way. Messianic License is a permission from Christ the Messiah not to fight violence with violence; it is permission to return love for hatred, and kindness for evil. Our era is the age of the Messiah.

He has taken over. We, his followers, are to do things his way. Violence begets violence. We are not to strengthen evil forces by violent opposition. We are to recognize what the violent do not, that we are all sons and daughters of the same Father.

Love overcomes. Christ overcame the world not by using his power as God so much as by subjecting himself out of love to his weakness as man. "When I am lifted up from the earth," he said, "I will draw everyone to myself." Cannot we all give witness that it is the tender love of his pierced heart, loving us despite all our sins against him, that makes him irresistible? And does he not call us to do for others what he did for us?

If we do not love others, we will not even love ourselves. A young person who was tempted to suicide managed to fight off the urge and make a trip to Fatima, and was transformed there. "Now," the youth wrote, "I love myself and other people more than I have ever before."

If we learn to forgive and love our enemy, we are given a great bonus. It teaches us to forgive and love even ourselves. It is ourselves we often have the most trouble forgiving. Even Judas, had he learned to love his enemies, would have been able to forgive himself, and ask Christ's forgiveness.

These are some of the mysteries of love which Jesus teaches. God lets his sun shine on the good and the bad, and makes the crops of both good and wicked farmers grow. He loves us all. He hates only wickedness. And God is our model. We are to pattern our love after his. Those who think they cannot are overlooking one fundamental fact. We are given the gift of God the Holy Spirit to make it possible. He is love. Nothing is hard or impossible to him.

"A" — Eighth Sunday of the Year

Is 49:14-15
1 Cor 4:1-5
Mt 6:24-34

PUTTING MONEY IN ITS PLACE

A monkey slipped his hand between the bars of his cage and grasped a piece of fruit, but found he couldn't draw his hand back as long as he kept clutching it. Too attached to the fruit to let go, he sat there a prisoner of greed. That monkey is an image of the greed Jesus condemns.

No man can serve two masters. You cannot give yourself to God and money. In saying that, our Lord is not discussing the need for money, but the greed for money. We need food, shelter, clothing, and medical care. We have in fact a responsibility to plan and set priorities, so we don't dissipate our resources on pleasures and trivia. People who fail in this responsibility are always living in crisis, and that is a vice, not a virtue.

Jesus is not discouraging work or planning; he is insisting on the need for a higher plan. We must plan to put God before all else. We must trust in God's plan more than our own. To do otherwise is to become addicted to money.

Many money addicts admit that God and his law come before money, but argue they have to make a few compromises in the "real world." They aren't any more aware of their money addiction than many excessive drinkers are of their alcohol addiction.

The money addict is recognized in the way he breaks God's commandments to serve his god, money.

When a money venture goes bad, he breaks the second commandment by cursing and swearing.

On Sundays he often breaks the third commandment because he's too busy about his ventures to attend Mass and rest from work.

When his parents need help, he is angry and annoyed and neglectful, thus breaking the fourth commandment.

The fifth commandment forbids murder and all harm to our neighbor. How many broken friendships, fistfights, and murders are committed over money? How many couples have an abortion to avoid spending money on a child?

The sixth commandment forbids adultery and all sexual sins. How many are greedy for money to buy sexual favors, or even to divorce and "buy" a more pleasing spouse?

The seventh commandment forbids stealing. Just as drug addicts so often steal to buy drugs, money addicts steal to get more money.

The eighth commandment forbids lying. How many lies are told to further a business deal or avoid paying a debt?

The ninth commandment forbids stealing another's wife. How many have used their money to win over a married person for whom they lusted?

The tenth commandment forbids us to look with greedy eyes on what others possess. The money addict is greedy for what his neighbor has, even though he has more than his neighbor.

We see how money enslaves, and we feel it too, for none of us fully escapes its lure. It gives lying promises about buying anything. But it can't buy health ruined by overwork, or sold honor or innocence or faithfulness or love or immortality. Its lies don't really fool us, but even so our greed goes on unless we love God above all things.

"I warn you, then," Jesus says, *"don't worry about your livelihood."* When Jesus says this, not all who drag their heels are money addicts. "What if there's plenty to worry about?" we murmur. Well, here we have to go back to what I said earlier. The Lord is not discouraging working and planning, only worrying. Working and planning serve us; worry is a mental distress that wastes our energies and produces unhappiness. Any good counselor would advise you to turn the wasted energies of worry to a more productive activity.

But Jesus has a further reason for warning against worry that can be brought out by a story. A passenger on a ship tossed by a bad storm saw a fearless little child playing contentedly, and asked in amazement, "Child, aren't you afraid?" And the child responded, "No. My daddy is the captain."

Jesus teaches us that our Father is Captain and Lord of History. His providence watches over us. It's as though Jesus said, "Worry is not only useless; it offends God because no power in creation can do anything to you that God does not allow."

I think we believe that, but a problem remains. We bite our fingers and think, "If we do what Jesus says, we're going to have a lot of hardships." Well, that's true. Jesus admits that each day has troubles enough. But if we try doing things our way, will our small, rebellious minds serve us better than the power, the wisdom and the love of God?

One young man anxious about his studies for the priesthood meditated on the Lord's command not to worry, and said, "Why worry, if you, my Commander in Chief, tell me not to?" He copied the words, "Do not worry," and set them out as a reminder whenever worry gnawed. His worrying gradually subsided until this command of Jesus changed his life. And it can change yours.

Have faith that your Father, the Lord of History, knows all your needs and watches over you. Not a fly drops without his permission. He loves you more than a mother loves her child. One day a tired priest, reading his Office, saw the words, "You are our God." He misread them, "We are your God." It sounded like blasphemy, but then he remembered that the great theologian, St. Thomas Aquinas, said that God loves us so much it is as if we were God's God. Doesn't the Incarnation and the crucifixion tell us as much? Then why don't we trust him?

We know in our hearts that true happiness lies not in being a slave of money but a friend of God. We don't really own anything; we administer it for God until he calls us home. We are part of God's provident care for others. God doesn't call everyone to become a poor monk. He employs many to serve him and his with what they possess. The Second Vatican Council says, "Christians, on pilgrimage toward the heavenly city, should seek and savor the things that are above. This duty in no way decreases, but rather increases, the weight of their obligation to work with all men in constructing a more human world."

If we are friends of God, we trust in God, and give to God, and so we are free to serve him and his with what we have. We are confident that he will shelter and feed us always, with a shelter and a food better than any this world dreams of.

"A" — First Sunday of Lent

Gn 2:7-9, 3:1-7
Rm 5:12-19
Mt 4:1-11

SECRETS OF THE DYING AND RISING OF CHRIST

Coconut lovers would soon become evident if we put out a big plate of coconut macaroons at one of our gatherings. During the Second World War, it was hard to find anything but *ersatz* coconut. You may remember the German word. It means *artificial*. To a coconut lover, the stuff was terrible; it tasted like soap.

Did it ever occur to you that temptation is an enticement to *ersatz* living, whereas God always calls us to the real thing? Adam and Eve learned that lesson the hard way. Lent is a trumpet call to abandon *ersatz* ways, and adopt the divine Son's true way, which passes through death and resurrection.

Let us probe the Lenten invitation along the following tracks: first, our Lord calls us, during this holy season, to his side to learn spiritual warfare; secondly, he calls us to live our baptismal likeness of him; and thirdly, he calls us to intensify our daily dying and rising with him.

First, then, our Lord calls us to learn spiritual warfare from him, our Commander in Chief. The first two readings are about spiritual warfare. Adam and Eve were seduced by *ersatz* living. They were tricked by the devil into believing they could do without God in their lives. The First Adam lost the war. The second reading tells of the Last Adam, coming to our rescue, entering into the same confrontations, temptations and battles as we, and showing the way to victory.

In today's Gospel, our Commander in Chief calls us to his side, to teach us himself. Adam lost our patrimony, and Christ regained it and more.

In "Praise to the Holiest," a hymn in the Lenten Liturgy of the Hours, we have this beautiful passage:

> O loving wisdom of our God!
> When all was sin and shame,
> A second Adam to the fight
> And to the rescue came.
> O wisest love! that flesh and blood
> Which did in Adam fail,
> Should strive afresh against the foe,
> Should strive and should prevail.
> And that a higher gift than grace
> Should flesh and blood refine,
> God's presence and his very self
> And essence all divine.

It was our flesh and blood that was battling there in the desert for those forty days, but it was sanctified not simply by grace, but by God himself joined to a human nature. Our great God-man and Lord battled for us. Can anyone who stands with him ever lose the war?

Secondly, Christ teaches us the life of baptism, of burial to that dying life of sin and rising to life in him. This is what we should hear today. On Ash Wednesday we were sprinkled with ashes. They signalled our dying to that sinful life which Adam and Eve espoused. Those ashes and this Lent call us to die to *ersatz* life, so that we may live eternal life. Adam's sin unleashed sin and death in the world; Christ's rejection of sin released eternal life.

Stop and reflect: What is temptation? Is it not always a call to a false and misconceived way of life? It's not always easy to tell the difference between the real thing and the false thing. The U.S. government is very concerned now because photocopiers are getting so good that soon someone may be able to photocopy money and pass out the fake bills as the real thing.

The deceivers have been good at spiritual photocopying since Adam and Eve. We need help to know the true way from the false. We need our divine Commander in Chief, and we need Peter and his successors, appointed by Christ to guide us in the way of his revelation. Temptation is always a deceitful inducement to reject God's way of nature and revelation and grace.

By rejecting God's way we sin mortally or venially. Mortal sin is a case of rejecting God's way in a grave matter, with serious reflection and full consent of the will. Venial sin is a case where the matter was lighter, or the reflection defective or the consent not really free.

Our Commander in Chief shows the way to penetrate the false promises of temptation and reject the rejections of God's way. Standing opposite to temptation is the call to grace, the call to the way of freedom, the way of the gifts of God. Jesus manifests this way in all its attractiveness. It is the way of faithfulness to love.

One day a man said, "What did we do to deserve this beautiful weather?" Another responded, "Nothing. It's a free gift. It's a grace." That is exactly what grace is — a free gift of God's love, of his help, of his forgiveness if we ask for it, of his way, his life, of union with him. The call, the help, and the inspiration to do good are all God's gift. The credit is his, but if we reject his grace, the sin is ours. As if they were gods, good parents experience this mystery with their children. They seem to provide them with everything, and yet children may turn out badly.

Finally, Lent is God's call to us his children to turn out well. He calls us to intensify our rejection of sin, and die to those things to which temptation entices us. He summons us to fast and reflect and pray with Jesus. The disciples of Jesus walked with him every day, and they learned every day. *We* are those disciples in our day. We should be learning from him daily. This season is a rededication to our baptismal commitment and way of life.

There is a sweetness to it, if we stay in the company of Jesus by prayer and meditation. With Jesus in the desert, we search out the ways to please the Father and serve his people. We learn not just what the Father is calling us to give up, but what he is calling us to take up, what he is calling us to be and do. With Jesus, we war against temptation and immorality. Let us commit ourselves to that with a good heart today.

In it all, Jesus will be at our side, and closer than our side. Within minutes, he will be within us in Holy Communion, and we will be one step closer to following him to eternal life in heaven, where there is no *ersatz* but only the real joy of God.

"A" — Second Sunday of Lent

Gn 12:1-4
2 Tm 1:8-10
Mt 17:1-9

THE STEEP CLIMB TO SANCTITY

Mount Tabor, a cone-shaped mountain on a plain near Nazareth, is where tradition places the transfiguration. It is a steep climb 2,400 feet into the sky. You can take a taxi, but not if you want to go up with Jesus!

St. Peter, reflecting what he saw there, called it the "holy mountain.'' Who could fail to see the holiness of Jesus there? The transfiguration was a fleeting disclosure of Jesus' holiness and a foretaste of his resurrection and a promise of our own.

Jesus labored up that steep ascent to arrive at his transfiguration. The climb of the three with him is symbolic of us all walking with Jesus up the ascent to holiness.

What is holiness and how do we come to it? God alone is holiness and the source of holiness. In yesterday's Gospel Jesus pointed the way to holiness in those stunning words, ''You must become perfected as your heavenly Father is perfect.''

How do we reduce those stunning words to any human measure and pattern that we can employ? The Greeks had the notion that ''Man is the measure of all things.'' How wrong they were! God appointed Moses to give sin-blinded human beings the Law as a measure and pattern for holiness. For God alone is the Measure and Measurer of all things.

Moses is there on the mountain to pass on his role of lawgiver to his foretold replacement. Jesus Christ is both the Lawgiver and the Law. By his Incarnation the Divine Model has been ''sifted to suit our sight.'' The Father says, ''This is my beloved Son in whom I am well pleased. Listen to him.'' Jesus is the explanation and refinement and final norm of interpretation for every human attempt to grow holy. One who ponders him and knows him knows best the true way to holiness. Jesus is the way and the truth and the life.

The way to holiness is the way of transfiguration with Christ. It begins with baptism. We died with Christ to live with Christ. Our new life is not something in the future. It is what we live daily. Like Jesus, we struggle to please the Father every day. Life and holiness are already in us. If God so willed, he could make our holiness flare out in a transfiguration even now — provided that we really have cultivated that holiness. In the Prayer after Communion, we will thank God for the holy mysteries which bring to us even in this life a share in the life to come.

Every time we act in love, attend Mass, receive a sacrament, or live in fidelity to Christ our Way by thought, word, or deed, we grow in holiness. Each time we faithfully carry out the duties of our state of life, we climb higher on Tabor.

The way is that of the cross. Moses and Elijah are there with Christ on Tabor discussing the passion he is to undergo in Jerusalem, as the prophets foretold. Do you think we can follow Christ and escape the cross? "Bear your share of the hardship which the Gospel entails," Paul exhorts us.

The way of holiness is the way of Christ loving and serving even to death on the cross. Abraham had the pain of leaving home, relatives and nation at the age of 75 to follow his call from God. Jesus endured worse. He had to remain with his people, and feel the pain, horror and terror of rejection and persecution and condemnation and death at the hands of those he loved. The pattern does not change. As long as there is sin and evil in the world, followers of the way of God will suffer from rejectors of the way, even from dear friends, as did Christ.

Christ summed up the commandments, the beatitudes and all the other norms of holiness by his way of love and faithfulness to the Father. That is the pattern of holiness and the pattern of Lent: Jesus praying, fasting, fighting temptation, serving, suffering, loving, dying. That is the way of sanctity.

We should now touch on the secrets of reaching sanctity. Every human pursuit has its "secrets of the trade." Sanctity is no exception. The expert and the genius in each trade are led by the right instincts and the secrets of the heart. In the field of sanctity we call them the saints.

The first secret is how to avoid one of the most common mistakes. A certain man fell badly into that common mistake. Fiery with zeal, he set about attacking and jailing those who disagreed with his version of the faith. Christ appeared to the man and showed him that, however sincere he was, he was sincerely wrong. And so Saul of Tarsus, purified, began to become the St. Paul we know. He learned to discern the spirits that moved him, and not judge any impulse holy until he found that it was true to all the norms of faith and love. Perhaps the ''sincerity'' that made him persecute Christians was built on a layer of self-deceit cloaking ambition or self-righteousness or just plain pride usurping the place of faith.

We must all discern the impulses that motivate us. Failure of many to do this in recent decades has put the Church on a virtual collision course with itself. We cannot count on Christ correcting us as he did Paul. He has given us the Church's teaching to measure all our thoughts, words and deeds, and speed us on the true way of the Lord.

There are many other secrets of sanctity based on the fact that ours is the religion of the Incarnation. Getting to know and love Christ is the shortest route of all, but it has many variations. Constant meditation on the passion of Christ has been called the science of the saints. Ardent devotion to the Sacred Heart of Jesus goes to the heart of the Incarnation, as does love of the Eucharist. One of the most noble, selfless, humble and hidden ways of sanctity is to seek and serve Christ in his least members: the most needy, despised and despaired of. Even the angels admire those who discover this way. And anyone who loves Mary ardently will find how swiftly she leads them to Jesus our holiness.

Find the way that best suits you, and you will run the way of sanctity with joy, as have so many before you.

''A'' — Third Sunday of Lent

Ex 17:3-7
Rm 5:1-2, 5-8
Jn 4:5-42

SAVED BY THE ''ENEMY''

A dentist told his priest-patient that he was once a dental surgeon, but switched to regular dentistry so he could save teeth, not pull them. He felt people don't like dentists because they hurt, but that he hurts only to heal. He refuses to let people neglect and lose their teeth, even if he loses some patients by doing what he must. When he goes home at night he wants to know he's done his patients good.

That dentist's experience parallels the experience of a faithful man of God. Moses did for the people what God required for their good. It wasn't easy for anybody. The people, fed up with hardship, asked, "Is the Lord with us or not?" They so took out their anger on Moses that he cried to God, "A little more and they will stone me!"

Just as people who neglect their teeth are enemies of their teeth, people who neglect the law of God are, in the word of St. Paul, "enemies" of God. But God's love for us is so great that no enmity can deter him from working for our salvation.

This truth is clear in the way Jesus treats the Samaritan woman he meets at Jacob's well. Samaritans were hostile to the Jews, and the Jews avoided them as heretics. Strange women were not spoken to by Jewish men. Jesus was keeping his Messianic identity secret for many reasons. Yet, to save this woman, he put aside conventions, proprieties, and the need to conceal his identity. The weary Good Shepherd sees a wounded and wayward sheep, and forgets all but her need. To the question, "Is God with us?" Jesus is saying "I Am" in word and deed.

A man of God must correct the sinner. The subtlety and gentle frankness with which Jesus does so is memorable. "Go, call your husband," he says. "I have none," the woman responds. "The fact is, you've had five," Jesus says, "and the man you're living with now is not your husband." Yet, knowing this, he has asked her for a drink of water. As she says, it is a request out of keeping with all the proprieties. She does not understand that he thirsts not for water, but to fulfill the Father's will that he give *her* living water.

There is water for the body; there is also water for the spirit, the living water of sanctifying grace. It flows from the Holy Spirit.

It gives divine life to our souls now, and immortality to our bodies at the resurrection.

When the rebellious people demanded water in the desert, Moses struck the rock, and water sprang forth. Christ, says St. Paul, is that rock. He was struck with a spear on Calvary, and the water of baptism and the blood of the Eucharist sprang forth.

By sin we commit enemy acts against God, but Jesus pursues his enemies not to kill but to heal, not to destroy but to save even at the cost of his life. "It is precisely in this that God proved his love for us," St. Paul says. While we were still enemies, Christ died for us.

Christ wants us to thirst for grace as people in parched lands thirst for water. At one time or another, we have all been parched with thirst, and known the longing for water. The thirst of the soul is greater, but not recognized for what it is. Many people mistake as thirst for pleasures and possessions their thirst for the living God and the water of the Holy Spirit.

St. Catherine of Siena is a saint who burned with thirst for grace. We are told that once she was meditating on the words of the Psalmist, "Create in me a clean heart, O Lord." She begged Christ her divine Spouse to take her heart and will and make them his. In the mystical experience that followed, Christ appeared to her, opened her side, took out her heart, and carried it away. Two days later he returned clothed in light, bearing in his hand a bright red heart with rays of fire. He opened her side, implanted it, and told her it was his own heart in place of hers. Centuries later, St. Margaret Mary had a similar experience.

Jesus' tender treatment of the woman at the well recalls these events. In this age of heart transplants, we should better realize the profound spiritual reality behind such a mystical exchange of hearts. The story of Eve taken from the side of Adam is explained by St. Paul and the Fathers of the Church as expressive of our baptismal origin from the pierced side of Christ. The Lenten liturgy is a 40-day symphony of baptism and its consequences. We are the body of Christ; the flow of grace from the Spirit of Christ is the blood in our veins.

A grasp on these mysteries gives us freedom. There is so much selfish clinging to things, but property as we know it is destined for extinction. There is so much unforgiveness, so much clinging to ancient hatred, even toward the Jews, though as Jesus himself said, ''Salvation is from the Jews.'' Christ nailed all such enmity to the cross by dying for his enemies. There is so much sin for sex, but sex as we know it is scheduled for obsolescence. Christ is the eternal bridegroom of his Church, and all love should be lived purely as part and parcel of his love for us all. Such love is not scheduled for extinction. It will grow until it fills heaven and earth. It is indistinguishable from grace, for it is part of grace, part of the outpouring of the Holy Spirit from the Heart of Christ.

''If today you hear his voice,'' the Psalmist says, ''harden not your hearts.'' The woman at the well did not. She understood that the Messiah wanted to save her, body and soul. So do we.

All of us sinners should take confidence from Jesus at Jacob's well. Even those in bad marriages, even those in the grip of sin and habits of sin, should take courage. Jesus does not turn away. God is in our midst. The grip of sin, which seems so powerful to us, is puny in his sight.

During Lent his bride the Church puts in our hands the weapons to fight all sin. Prayer, fasting and good works open us to receive the grace of Christ. That grace overcomes sin. It wins for us more than victory, as it did for the woman at the well. To this day, a visitor to Jacob's well can still draw water, as she did; and grace from Christ, as did she.

"A" — Fourth Sunday of Lent   1 S 16:1, 6-7, 10-13
                                                     Ep 5:8-14
                                                     Jn 9:1-41

ENDING ALL THE DARKNESS

When darkness descends, a stranger in a strange land cannot find his way. Without light, he is like a blind man. Life itself is that strange land, for around the corner lie all our tomorrows, and we do not know what they will bring. We need a shepherd who can see them, and will lead us. That shepherd is Christ. We need the light by which we can share his vision, and that light is faith.

But light gives us more than sight. We city dwellers may forget what a farmer always remembers, that plants have no eyes, but they too need light. By light they grow and produce. Without light, even the towering redwoods could never be. The sun is their light of life.

Christ, our sun, radiates the light of faith into our minds and the life of grace into our souls. He summons us from the tomb of sin and death into the daylight of his life.

Last week, the Lenten liturgy expressed the mystery of baptism through the figure of life-giving water; this week it manifests the mystery of baptism under the figure of light.

A man born blind sits in his darkness, a figure of all born of Adam. Christ comes, mixes his spittle with the soil from which Adam was taken, and anoints those unseeing eyes. The man washes his eyes in the pool of Siloam, and sees.

We were rubbed with the oil of anointing, and immersed in the pool of baptism. We came out seeing with the eyes of faith, and living by the light that is life.

We may think we see better than we do. The man born blind was too thrilled to realize how little he saw when first his eyes were opened. It was not until Jesus revealed himself as the one to be believed in, and the man said, "I do believe, Lord," that Jesus opened his eyes to see heaven as well as earth.

Our eyes are only half open until we see that the Good News of the Gospel does not consist in the Sermon on the Mount or the message of love, but in the person of Jesus. He is the Good News. He is our Shepherd and our luminous way.

We may not realize how Jesus has illumined the very nature of religion. Religion before Jesus generally fell into one or other of two errors. It was either mired in materialism, or it despised the flesh in the name of the spirit.

The Greeks generally fell into materialism. Despairing of attaining to God as pure spirit, they pictured their gods in the likeness of humanity with all the same foibles and lusts.

The smaller number who attained to some contact with God as pure spirit tended to despise their own bodies as below their dignity. This Christ rejected, and so St. Augustine could write, "Anyone who extols the nature of the flesh as evil is as carnal in his love for the soul as he is in his hatred for the flesh, because his thoughts flow from human vanity and not from divine truth." In other words, such people despise what God called "very good."

The religion Jesus taught loves body and soul, and God who made both. In Jesus, God himself took flesh to tell us anew of its goodness. We love Jesus in his humanity and his divinity. Taught by him, we love our own humanity as men and women; and brought to it by him, we share in his divinity by grace.

Religion in Jesus teaches us to seek the light of God's will as our true good, whereas pagan peoples sought to guide themselves by their own darkness, and do their own will.

God chose David, a shepherd boy, as a prefigurement of Christ our true king. Why David, and not one of his seven brothers? God explains the reason when he says, "I have found David, a man after my own heart, who will do all my will."

Christ was the true David doing God's will. On coming into the world he said, "Sacrifice you did not desire of me, but to do your will." He taught us to pray, "Father, your will be done." Facing his death, he said, "Not what I will, but what you will."

Our well-being lies in doing the same. St. Augustine wrote, "This is in fact the difference between good men and bad men, that good men make use of the world in order to enjoy God, whereas bad men would like to make use of God in order to enjoy the world."

We can all fall into that error of bad men. In Sigrid Undset's great novel *Kristin Lavransdotter,* Kristin, wife and mother, discovers this truth at age 50:

> "Never, it seemed to her, had she prayed to God for
> aught else than that he might grant her her own will . . .
> And now she sat here with a bruised spirit — not
> because she had sinned against God, but because she
> had been granted to follow the devices of her own heart
> to the journey's end."

Our eyes are not fully open until we see that true happiness lies in the enjoyment of God, and true delight in the merging of our wills with his.

Our eyes of faith are fully open when at last we embrace even our afflictions as something God permits only to glorify us the more. In the death the Father called him to accept, Jesus foresaw the flood of love it would win from a grateful world.

One man passed through hell and back in his battles with alcoholism. Even though he was a priest, it was only with the help of Alcoholics Anonymous that he learned to surrender himself to God and find the strength of sobriety. After that, he was for years a help and comfort to an army of alcoholics. Then he was taken to the hospital with blood clots. Having learned how God brought good even out of his troubles he could say to a fellow priest, "I spent a half hour in prayer. I thanked God for all his favors to me, and accepted whatever he plans for me." Within a week he had gone home to the Father.

Strengthened by faith, we rush toward Easter, the feast which tells how the Father brings good from evil, and how he loves both body and soul and plans eternal life for both. But even on the road to Easter, there are stops for refreshment. The greatest of them is the Eucharist. We plan to stop there today, and taste the resurrection Easter celebrates.

"A" — Fifth Sunday of Lent

Ezk 37:12-14
Rm 8:8-11
Jn 11:1-45

NO WAITING FOR LIFE

Who has not experienced the grief and sorrow that the death of Lazarus awoke in Jesus and all his dear friends? His sisters are near collapse. His friends are supporting them with tearful hearts. But in their midst is the Christ who changes everything. As man, he wept for Lazarus; as God, he raised him from the dead, and turned a companionship of sorrow into a fellowship of unbounded joy.

Our funerals should reflect the Lazarus event. Sorrow there must be, when we are parted from a loved one. Joy there should be, for our friend has gone on to the life we long for.

A young college student was killed in a car accident. His faith-filled family and friends gathered for the Mass. Tears of love flowed in streams. But with the experience of that strong, selfless love came "intimations of immortality" which confirmed faith, and cast out despair and the fear of death.

The death of a relative or friend is an unmatched opportunity to give help and support. Grief supported on all sides by the arms of love is suffused with a purifying sweetness. It is lifted beyond itself by the incense of hope which all love breathes into the air. Unlike Jesus, we cannot restore life, but we can give witness to the undying life in us, and our hope of resurrection. In this climate of love, grief neither crushes nor mires us; it is turned into a purifying experience from which we come forth better and tenderer persons.

A woman wrote to her brother about the many Mass cards she received from friends of their mother, who was a much-loved woman. She expressed hope that through all the Masses their mother would be well up in the mansions of God. Then she added, "Hope she's having a great reunion with friends and family." This is the difference Christ makes. He is our hope because he is our Resurrection.

But at that Lazarus resurrection, Christ spoke a word to console us not just at times of death, but during every day of our mortality. He did not say, "I *will* be the life," but "I *am* the life." He is not our life only in some vague future; he is our life now and in the future. It is a clear and solemn teaching of the Scriptures and the Church that once we are baptized in Christ and, all the more, receive his risen body in the Eucharist, we live by Christ's life always. If we pray enough, we even experience his presence.

When we see a little child, we rarely recall the fact that he or she already possesses the power to grow into manhood or womanhood. It is only a matter of time and growth. So, too, baptism and Eucharist have already implanted in us the power to live forever. In the Preface for the Mass of the dead, we say, "Lord, for your faithful people, life is changed, not ended." Death is the loss only of bodily life. This is what Jesus was telling us when he said to Martha, "Whoever is alive and believes in me will never die." The body will die, but not the person. And the person's body will be restored at the resurrection.

Why do so many disbelieve in eternal life, and what can they do about it? Well, consider this: Eternity is defined as the endless, total, and simultaneous possession of life. Only God fulfills that definition. And since it doesn't take a genius to see that created things change and decay, many people disbelieve in eternal life. But now recall what Jesus said to Martha: "I *am* the resurrection and the life." In other words, he is saying that we can have resurrection and eternal life only by being joined to his Godhead. That is the solution to the difficulty. Those who believe him have no problem. For as Paul says, neither angels nor men nor life nor death can separate us from Christ.

Let us, however, admit that one person and one thing *can* separate us from Christ. The one person is the self, and the one thing is mortal sin. Death is from sin and a figure of sin. Sin kills both body and soul, and destroys the life Christ planted in us. Mortal sin is more grievous than all else. It is to be avoided at all cost, and repaired with all speed by the sacrament of penance. The raising of a dead sinner in confession is a greater act of God's power than the raising of Lazarus.

Mortal sin involves grievous matter, sufficient reflection, and full consent of the will. It involves choosing something other than God when there is a choice between something and God.

God's word and his Church tell us what sins are mortal. That is the only reliable way to find out, for who can tell us what offends God but God? Few people ever realize how that knowledge frees us. Some religions say it is a sin not only to abuse alcoholic beverages, but to use them at all. There is a religion that says it is a sin to kill a cow. Through the ages many religions have condemned quite innocent pleasures under the ban of sin. But we are freed by the teaching of Christ from such mistakes and superstitions. All the more, then, should the impulse of gratitude help us to live gladly the law of Christ.

Pilgrims to the little town of Bethany are shown the tomb which tradition holds to be the place where Lazarus lay. You can be sure there is a sense of resurrection at that shrine. But we have a better shrine of resurrection. On our altar, at the consecration, we have Christ himself, the resurrection and the life. Let us offer him to the Father in the Holy Sacrifice of redemption, the renewal of the mystery of Calvary. Then we will receive him, and once again become ourselves the shrine and the promise of resurrection.

When Jesus went to Bethany for Lazarus' sake, Thomas

recognized the danger. Bethany was a suburb of Jerusalem, and the authorities there were hostile to Jesus. So Thomas exclaimed with fear and devotion, "Let us go and die with him!" In a sense, that is exactly what we have to do. St. Paul says we have to make our bodies die to their sinful desires if we are to live in Christ. Lent is an intensified call to do that dying.

Still, it is better to accent the positive. St. Thomas, who saw the resurrection, would have no quarrel with us if we adopted his statement with the change of one word: "Let us go and live with him!"

"A" — Passion Sunday

Mt 21:1-11
Is 50:4-7
Ph 2:6-11
Mt 26:14-27:66

A WEEK WITH CHRIST

After a rainstorm, strollers in the hills and mountains of north Georgia, near the headwaters of the Chattahoochee, can find semiprecious stones washed to the surface. Most do not. They can't distinguish them from the many intermingled stones and pebbles, so they trample underfoot the jewels that could be theirs. Similarly, our walk through Passion Week can unearth many treasures, but how many recognize and claim the precious and brilliant jewels of grace that can be theirs?

Certain days and events stand out from the sweep of history: the day the wheel was fashioned; the day Columbus discovered America; the hour the first man walked on the moon; the moment of the first nuclear explosion.

For the believer, however, these events are mere foothills before the high Alps of Passion Week, the greatest week in history. At the Last Supper, Christ instituted the Holy Sacrifice, which will be offered from the rising to the setting of the sun until the sun sets no more. He gave us his body and blood in the Eucharist, promised the gift of the Holy Spirit, revealed his divine indwelling, and gave us the new commandment of love. On the morrow, he suffered his passion, and redeemed the world. And on the third day beyond, he rose from the dead to provision us with bodily life that will never die. These events, though part of time, have eternal consequences.

How can we make these consequences our own in the course of Passion Week? A story will suggest the answer. Once a man named Bill pointed down into the Florida waters and said, "Look at those fish!" Josh, his companion, said, "I don't see them. How can you see them?" Some days later they were walking through a field. Josh reached down, picked a few wild strawberries, and ate them. Bill said, "I didn't notice any strawberries. How did you see them?" Josh responded, "The same way you saw the fish!"

We can make the consequences of Passion Week ours the way Bill learned to spot fish, and Josh, strawberries, and the way some in the Georgia hills learn to recognize and collect semiprecious stones. Why be deprived of the riches of Christ that this neighbor or that will be amassing this week? Christ died to have each of us amass his riches.

It's not really hard to amass them, though it takes some effort and practice and sacrifice. Christ said to pray always, and never lose heart. This is the week to begin. The prayer of Holy Week consists in walking with Christ. Read and ponder the Gospel accounts of the Passion in the coming days. Turn your thoughts to Jesus frequently during the week. Ask yourself what he was doing at this day and hour of his final week on earth, and reflect on it.

Be with him at the banquet in Bethany six days before Passover. See Mary of Bethany pouring the oil over his head as a symbol of his burial. Hear the traitor condemn "wasting" the money for that ointment which will never be forgotten.

Walk in spirit with Jesus the next day as he makes his triumphal entry into Jerusalem, cheered by a vast crowd of people, and wonder which of them will be among the mob howling for his blood before the week is out. Realize that to sin is to stand with those who do.

Hear him preaching in the temple area during these last days of his life, watch him casting out the business going on that had no right there, and ask if any illicit business is going on in the temple of body and soul.

Sit with him at table on his last night, as he pours out his deepest love and choicest gifts. Try to take them in as never before.

Be with him in his agony, though the others sleep. Recall how, centuries later, he asked St. Margaret Mary to make a weekly hour of reparation to his Sacred Heart for the love that is lacking still.

Follow him dragged through the night to Caiaphas, to prison, past Peter denying him. See Pilate trying to evade the issue by parading him off to Herod, and Herod mocking him and parading him back. Gaze at his bloody scourging and scornful crowning, and condemnation to death, and gruelling way of the cross. Ask who is willing to be the Simon of Cyrene of our day, helping him to carry the burden.

See him stripped and thrown on the cross, his sacred limbs tortured by the pounded nails. Then watch as he hangs in agony through the crawling hours, and listen for his last deep words.

Ponder the fact that this suffering is not the collapse of Christ's endeavors, as the disciples thought, but the completion of his work, and the fulfillment of the Father's plan. Every saint has shared Jesus' passion as well as his ascent to glory, and we will be no exception. Beside his cross, we learn to bear our own sufferings, so small compared with his. We learn with him abandonment to divine providence.

While men crucify him on earth, see angels adoring him in heaven, and recall the greatness of our God and Savior.

"Were you there when they crucified my Lord?" Say "Yes, I was there. In prayer I stood with Mary and the Magdalene and

John.'' By prayer we can be there. We can count his wounds if they can be counted. We begin to see that unless we are there often we can never realize the greatness of what we offer in the Mass. Even if we ask the Father for the world in return, how can we ask too much? And if these truths register, we will yearn to be with Christ each day in the liturgies of Holy Week.

We see Our Lady throb with grief as his slain body is laid in her arms; we feel our loss as he is laid in the tomb. We accompany her to her lodgings, silent in respect for a sorrow too deep for words.

Walk with Christ in Passion Week. Tread none of his gifts into the mire. Find more than semiprecious stones. If we spend the week with him, on Easter we can hope to have the tumult of joy that should be ours, and bring to the risen Christ in the Eucharist the love that should be his.

"ABC" — Easter Sunday

Ac 10:34, 37-43
Col 3:1-4
Jn 20:1-9

EASTERING WITH JESUS

One Saturday before Easter, a priest aboard a plane saw a sweet little girl in her mother's arms gazing at him from the seat ahead. He exchanged a happy smile with her, then got to work on his Easter homily. Suddenly there was a commotion under the seat in front of him and to his right. And there was that sweet little girl bursting unexpectedly into his life. All on her own, she had decided on a visit. The next day she appeared in his homily as a symbol of that fresh Easter life of Christ coming into the lives of us all. He too comes in unexpected ways, as he came into the lives of his disciples on the first Easter Sunday.

All of a sudden, Jesus was there among them again in his risen body. From then on, their lives were changed. A realization of how much they were changed will be helped by a brief reflection.

Through the ages the whole of humankind remained huddled on a little island of life surrounded by the boundless sea of death. One by one, each person slipped into that sea and was never heard from again.

Then came the man who said he would return out of that dark sea on the third day, carrying in his body the gift of undying life for us all, as the prophets had said. On the first Good Friday, that man's body lay mangled and dead, as he had prophesied.

On the third day, there was excitement and terror, an earthquake, angels, an empty tomb. Then there was Jesus, and the women took hold of his risen body and worshipped, and the men sat and ate with him. They never knew where they were going to meet him next or in what way he would come into their lives, in his person or through the person of others in whom he lived.

That excitement has never ceased, and that new hope awakened has never abated. What Easter celebrates is the faith that Christ has died, Christ has risen, Christ comes into our lives.

The readings at the Easter Mass tell how the risen Christ came into the lives of the first disciples. The faith tells us how he comes into our lives. The central way is through the Holy Sacrifice of the Mass. Jesus uses the Mass in union with the bloody sacrifice of Calvary to take away our sins; he uses the banquet of the Mass to come to each of us. We gather at Mass not just to recall how he came to others, but to have him come to us. Easter is the day of days to stir up our faith and meet Jesus in the Eucharist.

In the Mass, Jesus Easters with his Church. Through the Mass, he gives his Church rebirth, nourishes it, and brings it joy. From the Holy Father on down, the Church is us.

In the second reading of the Easter Mass, St. Paul uses the phrase, "Christ our life." That life of Christ in us is the focal point of baptism and Eucharist and Church and Easter. When Christ promised the Eucharist he said, "He who eats my flesh and drinks my blood has everlasting life, and I will raise him up on the last day." Through the mystery of the Eucharist, the Resurrection is ours.

There is another mystery that is rarely mentioned. Jesus said, "He who eats my flesh and drinks my blood lives on in me and I in him." Does he not, then, continue to Easter in us once we receive him, as long as we don't drive him away by mortal sin?

Of Mahatma Gandhi, Pandit Nehru said, "Where he sits is a temple and where he walks is hallowed ground." How much more could we say that of Mary? And we can say it of each of us, because Christ has promised to make us his home and his temple.

There are consequences to all of this. St. Paul, reminding us that we "have been raised up with Christ," cries out, "Be intent on things above rather than on things of earth."

Just what does he mean? Is he telling us to abandon our earthly responsibilities? Far from it! Hopefully, Christians know Paul better than that. Long before, when the disciples stood gawking up to where Jesus had ascended into heaven, the angels said, "Why are you standing there looking at the sky?" The angels were telling them it was time they got on with their lives.

Actually, Paul spells out the "things above" on which we are to be intent. He tells us to put on the heavenly garments of "heartfelt compassion, kindness, humility, gentleness, and patience, bearing with one another and forgiving one another." We are to wear these heavenly garments here on Earth as Jesus did.

After all, if we have his life, we ought to really live his life as ours. Like him, we ought to go around doing good, free of sin, and helping to free others from sin by our prayer and service and example. Since we are the "children of the resurrection," having our treasure in heaven with Jesus, we are free to live on earth without clinging to anything earthly. That is the way we will be sure to arrive at the glory of the resurrection promised by Easter and the Eucharist.

If there is any day when our hearts should turn to the hope of resurrection, and long for it, this is the day. If we love Jesus, how can we not long to be with him? If he has taught us of God the Father, how can we not long to come home to him? If he has taught us of the Holy Spirit of love, how can we not want to see and drink of that torrent of love forever?

Every year, on Easter, the patriarch of Jerusalem goes to the tomb of Jesus, hard by Calvary. In union with bishops and priests from all over the world, he concelebrates Mass with the faithful from nations around the globe. And there, where he rose, Jesus returns in the mystery of the Eucharist.

The place where we celebrate Mass is different, but the mystery is the same. By our presence at Mass, we are saying, "Easter with us, Lord Jesus!" And he does.

"A" — Second Sunday of Easter

Ac 2:42-47
1 P 1:3-9
Jn 20:19-31

YESHUA YAHWEH

Human beings are strange creatures. Many are deaf both to God's word and to the evidence before their eyes that suffering and sickness are sin's product. They say, "If there were a God, he would halt the suffering and sickness, and do some tremendous deed." When told he did such a deed, that he raised Jesus from the dead to be our life, they say, "I don't believe it!"

"The resurrection," says St. Augustine, "is God's supreme and wholly marvelous work." It is so marvelous that Thomas the Apostle didn't believe at first, either. But in accord with the saying that "Freedom is nothing but a chance to be better," he changed his mind. And what a change! He soared up to the clearest profession of the Godhood of Jesus found in the Bible: "My Lord and my

God.'' He is the first to join the revealed name for the Savior, *Yeshua,* Jesus, to the revealed name for God, *Yahweh.* He confessed our Savior to be Yeshua-Yahweh, Jesus-God.

So Thomas won out, but he never fell into the triple error of those unbelievers with whom I began. Each of them tries to solve all his religious problems alone; each fails to see himself as a partial cause of the troubles he laments; and each fails to see that God intends him to be a partial solution as well.

In this Sunday's first reading, we are brought into the presence of the Church at its founding. Like us, the first Christians clung to the teaching of the apostles, met in fellowship, broke the bread of the Eucharist together, and praised God for salvation in Jesus. But if strikingly like us, they were also strikingly different. They sold what they had and shared everything in common.

Has the Church lost that first fervor? Does anyone wish he could be part of it? Then listen to the three degrees of it which still exist in the Church.

A young man was told by his dentist, who had the unlikely name of Dr. Plesur, that ''You Catholics have the real communists. The members of your religious orders share everything in common.'' He was right. The priests, sisters and brothers of religious orders own nothing personally. Like the early Church, they give all they have and earn to their communities. That first fervor lives on in religious life.

And there is another form of sharing. In the early 1970's, a group of married couples who had fallen away from their religious faiths decided to found a commune and share everything. They wanted a drug-free environment for their children. After a while, they studied the religions of the world together, and decided that if God loved us, he would become one of us, as Christians teach. So they became non-denominational Christians. Then, when the Supreme Court issued the Roe vs. Wade decision legalizing abortion, that family-loving commune was horrified. They decided that the Christian branch which taught that abortion was an abomination would be the true Church. After an investigation, they entered the Catholic Church. They allied themselves with the Dominicans, and became the St. Martin de Porres Dominican Community of New Hope, Kentucky. Like the early Christians, they are families who share all things in common.

Besides the religious orders and the New Hope community of families, every Christian and every family is called to give of what they have to the needy. Catholic Charities appeals are part of every parish. So, in these three ways the Church keeps alive the fervor of the early Church.

But there is a further way of keeping this fervor alive. Every truly Christian family shares family life and possessions with the generosity Christ's love inspires. Selfishness in family life is contrary to everything Christ stands for. Generosity and *forgiveness* are essentials of family life.

That brings us to the spirit of forgiveness which Jesus raised to new heights by his teaching, and to newer heights still when he came after the resurrection. It was on that first Easter eve that he gave his priests the power to forgive sin. "Receive the Holy Spirit. If you forgive men's sins they are forgiven them." By that sacrament of reconciliation, Jesus gave his Church the power to establish peace between God and us, and between ourselves. To neglect that sacrament is to neglect peace.

Sometimes we need the experience of outsiders to appreciate, by their lack, what the faith gives us. When Mother Teresa of Calcutta spoke on Japanese TV about the evils of abortion, she assured people that God was a forgiving God, and would forgive abortion as well. From then until midnight, weeping women kept phoning, expressing their gratitude for her assurance of God's loving forgiveness. So, as we recall how Jesus risen gives us the sacrament of forgiveness he won for us on the cross, we ask this question: If we neglect confession, if we are not mindful of our faults and sins, and are not repeatedly experiencing God's forgiveness, will even family members be readily forgiving toward one another? And without forgiving hearts, do not families drift apart, and even fall apart?

Thomas the Apostle came close to illustrating how members of the family of the Church can drift apart, and even fall away. His absence from the assembly when Jesus came on Easter struck his faith a terrible blow. All were anguished at being divided on that most basic touchstone of faith, the resurrection.

Does not absence from the assembly at Sunday Mass lead to like problems? The habitually absent fail to grow in faith with the rest. They fail to meet the risen Jesus in the Mass and the Eucharist. Faith weakens, knowledge of the faith clouds over, and divisions multiply. How can it not happen, when instead of breaking the bread of heaven together, they break God's commandment to keep holy the Sabbath day? Thomas was absent one Sunday, and his loss almost overwhelmed him. Let us be present with our fellow believers every Sunday, to say, with Thomas, to the risen Jesus at the consecration, "My Lord and my God."

"A" — Third Sunday of Easter

Ac 2:14, 22-28
1 P 1:17-21
Lk 24:13-35

RECOGNIZING JESUS

Seven miles northeast of Jerusalem stands the quiet little town of El Qubeiba. Enter the church there, walk down the central nave, and find Jesus clad in a rose-colored robe, sitting at table breaking bread. The two seated with him are forever stunned with recognition. "It is the Lord!"

Modern El Qubeiba is, by our best calculations, the ancient town of Emmaus. The sacred meal depicted in the sculpture is taking place on the Sunday eve of the first Easter. The two disciples frozen into stone commemorate the moment they recognized the risen Jesus.

When we first meet these two in today's Gospel, they are men in despair. As the account proceeds, hope stirs; as it ends, they race off in possession of the world's desire.

We come together each Sunday to repeat their experience. By faith we hope to recognize the risen Christ in our midst. So let us ask questions: How did their transformation take place? What must we do to rise in hope with them? Will we recognize Jesus at Mass today? We may not, unless we enter into the experience as they did. So let's pay at least as much attention to their story as we would to a good whodunnit yarn.

They were on a journey. So are we. The first reading urges us to conduct ourselves reverently during our "sojourn in a strange land." And just as they walk along with hopes dashed, so we bring our troubles with us to Mass.

They had hoped for so much from this Jesus of Nazareth. Why had they become men of despair? Jesus explains why. He says, "What little sense you have! How slow you are to believe!" Despite being his disciples, they had understood neither his crucifixion nor the power of God. They did not grasp what St. Peter explains in the first reading, that Jesus was delivered up by "the set purpose and plan of God." Nor did they understand that the Holy Spirit had foretold in Psalm 16 that corruption would never lay claim to the Messiah's body. Die he had to, but only to deliver us all by pouring out "the blood of a spotless, unblemished lamb chosen before the world's foundation." Then he would rise again as both he and the prophets had foretold.

Like the Emmaus two, we will not understand unless we make the same intense effort as they to grasp what really took place on Calvary. They did not succeed even then, until they listened to the Lord's own explanation. That same explanation is given us throughout the New Testament readings we hear at Mass.

Just as those two disciples failed to realize that Christ's death on Calvary was the sacrifice of salvation, we can fail to realize that the Mass is the sacrifice of Calvary renewed. Do not some see the Mass as simply a holy service and a holy meal?

It is a holy meal, but a holy meal was often the final episode of a Jewish sacrifice. Examine the Book of Leviticus. See the many sacrifices which end in sharing with God at table the animal victim just sacrificed by the priest. The first Christians, Jews all, would think we have lost our roots if we don't know the connection. Don't we hear at the consecration of every Mass the words of Jesus offering his body and blood for us in holy sacrifice? Pope Paul VI called the Mass "a sacrifice, a memorial and a banquet."

In the separate consecration of bread and wine, Jesus put before us a symbol of the separation of his body and blood on Calvary. He died to carry out the Father's will, and his obedience is the essence of his sacrifice.

The two on the Emmaus road listened intently to Jesus, and began to catch a glimmer of the mystery of Calvary. Their hearts began to burn with love. So will ours, if we grasp the word of God at Mass. When the bread is broken, we, like them, will exclaim, "It is the Lord!" And as they must have taken into their hands with indescribable reverence the bread he had blessed, so will we reverently receive the bread of his risen body.

But let me say again: Our faith may fail to recognize Jesus in the Mass if we do not ponder his passion, death, and resurrection, and then live what we ponder. "Believers know the body of Christ," says St. Augustine, "if they do not fail to be the body of Christ." If we ponder the sufferings in his life, and accept those in ours, we will recognize Jesus when he enters our life. And if we do recognize Jesus at Mass, we will give the same evidence of it that Cleopas and his companion gave. They rushed out to broadcast what they had learned. It is impossible to keep the Good News pent up once our hearts have caught the fire of the Heart of Christ.

Now let me tell the Emmaus story as it never happened, thank God. At least, it didn't happen to Cleopas and his companion this way, but perhaps it did to many others. As they reached the Emmaus turnoff, the stranger who had joined them made as if he were going on. They thought, "He shouldn't be traveling this robber-infested road alone so late. But if we invite him to join us, we may have to pay for his lodgings, and we're pretty tight for money." So they bid the stranger goodbye — and go up to to eat their supper alone. The Gospel certainly implies that this would have happened if they had not pressed him to share their food and shelter.

We should think that over. Christ said, "What you do to others you do to me." If we do not invite Christ into our lives daily by kindness to the persons with whom we live and associate, we will be living that second version of the Emmaus story. We may go to Mass and receive Christ in the Eucharist, but we will not really be inviting him into our lives. Should we be surprised, then, if we do not recognize him in the Eucharist?

On that road to Emmaus, the Good Shepherd went looking for his stray sheep, found them, and brought them home. If any of us has strayed, he is on our road today. He censured them for failing to think and to believe. He is saying to all of us, "Open your heart to me. Open it even wider." If we do that, we will recognize him with joy in the breaking of bread.

"A" — Fourth Sunday of Easter

Ac 2:14, 36-41
1 P 2:20-25
Jn 10:1-10

WHERE ARE THE YEARLING SHEPHERDS?

From the prophets of old to the Indian guides of frontier days to the psychologists of our day, guides and counselors have played a crucial role in human life. A good career guide can save wasted years, a wise marriage counselor a marriage; a medical adviser can save a life, a caring priest a soul.

The Guide of guides is the Good Shepherd. How often people go to other counselors when they really need their Shepherd!

The readings of this Sunday speak about shepherds; Jesus too speaks of them in the Gospel. And so at once we think of the Good Shepherd. But that can distract us from what Jesus is really saying. He is not saying here that he is the Good Shepherd, but that he is the sheepgate.

The image doesn't sound attractive, and little attention is paid to it. Still, in using it, Jesus is making a greater claim than where he calls himself the Good Shepherd. In calling himself the Good Shepherd, Jesus leaves room for lesser shepherds; but in calling himself the sheepgate, he leaves no room at all. "All who came before me," he says, "are thieves and marauders." Strong language. It prompts us, in this season of his resurrection, to ask ourselves, "Who but Jesus ever gave proof of being the Gate to resurrection and the source of our rebirth as children of God?" Unless we pass through this sheepgate, we will never enter the pasture of eternal life.

This sheepgate parable invites us to think of the shepherds he appoints to lead his sheep to him. At the head of these stand the priests, from the Pope to the humblest country pastor. Priests are in short supply. Some flocks are without shepherds. It is a dangerous thing for a flock. And since our seminaries are not half full, it will get worse. Some countries are in worse straits than we. If all our priests went to serve in South America, it would lack priests still. Planet earth is a pasturage of sheep without shepherds. Young men should hear this, and listen for the privileged call to be Christ's shepherd.

Why the shortage? Who is failing? To come to the answer, we have to stop seeing priests as the only shepherds. Let us call the other shepherds by name.

Mothers and fathers are the first and most necessary shepherds of their children. Each home is a little parish. Pope Pius XII said that "examples of domestic virtues have such efficacy that families may, in a certain manner, be called the first seminaries, the first novitiates." But God knows that parents need the help of religious sisters and brothers, and all good teachers. They too shepherd us to the sheepgate. Many a Catholic owes his faith to them, and many a priest his vocation.

Vocational research highlights both the successes and the failures of each of these kinds of shepherds. One survey reported that 45 percent of priests and 55 percent of sisters traced their vocation back to other priests and sisters. This only concurs with the life principle that every living thing begets its like. A priest is meant to be, as the First Letter of Peter says, the pattern for the flock. Unless he forms his whole flock into a priestly people, he is not likely to inspire priestly vocations.

Where do we priests fail? The Synod of Bishops pointed out one area of failure: The priest must do more than preach the Gospel and offer the Holy Sacrifice. Like Jesus, he must work for a "more just secular order." If he fails to treat of the burning social issues of poverty, peace, inadequate housing, and abortion, he is likely to strike teenagers as a perhaps likeable, but useless ascetic. He must move his people to work for a better society, as the prophets and saints have done from the beginning.

But in the end the priest-shepherd can only build on what the other shepherds have done. Parents and teachers spend far more hours with the young than the priest. They make or break vocations. In families where love of God and wisdom and goodness flourish, vocations sprout. Where families chase the dollar sign, vocations can no more sprout than plants in stones. Surveys indicate that bad parental example kills vocations.

One boy spontaneously wrote letters to a priest he had never met about his secret desire to be a priest. After a time, he wrote in shock that he had mentioned that secret desire to his father. "You'd think that I had killed someone," was the way he described his father's reaction. What if St. John's father had reacted that way to John's following of Jesus, and deprived John of his glory as an apostle? Pope Pius XII said that "Parents should put aside their fears in this matter and by daily example of Christian life attempt to bring about the greatest honor they will ever possess."

God appoints parents to take his place as shepherds of their children. Parents should ponder Psalm 23, "The Lord is my Shepherd," and wonder whether they inspire their children to think of them as faithful and loving shepherds. Do they fill their children's every need, provide refreshment and repose, guide them in right paths, and keep them from straying ways?

Today's readings recall the shepherd feeding his sheep. At Mass, the Good Shepherd feeds us on the feast of love. All who love his feast know that he who gave it also gave the priesthood. It was his will to give only the ordained priest the power to act in his person to bring about the sacrifice and the banquet.

Isn't it evident, then, that Jesus wants all who love the Mass — not to mention our Holy Mother the Church — to do all they can to stir priestly vocations? What can be done? Pray, lead a holy life, live by the teaching of the Holy Father, get involved in God's work in the Church. Respect priests, even those who do not live up to their calling. A priest's greatness lies not in himself but in the indispensable role God gives him. Do these things, and send a message to the young, a message of faith, without which there can be no vocations. The message is that God is the One Thing Necessary, that we can never give him enough, and that those who give all to him and his people are the most blessed of all. They are, most clearly, the children of the resurrection.

"A" — Fifth Sunday of Easter   Ac 6:1-7
                                                                 1 P 2:4-9
                                                                 Jn 14:1-12

DEACONS RESTORED

Good historical writings are a window opening into the past, by which we can see forming the very world we have inherited. The Gospel readings for the fifth Sunday of Easter are a window into our Jewish origins. They illuminate with inspired brilliance the mystery of our Catholic priesthood, and how and why it branched off into the diaconate.

At the Last Supper, Jesus ordained his apostles the first ministerial priests, and appointed them to offer his Eucharistic Sacrifice. But, as St. Peter says to us all in the second reading of this Sunday, "You are a chosen race, a royal priesthood." By baptism, all Christians share priestliness.

Today's first reading opens a window into the moment when this fundamental priesthood branched off into the form of priestly service called the diaconate. The setting is not long after Jesus' Ascension. The Church is just sprouting into being. In fact, at the time, the Church appeared to be simply that part of the Jewish synagogue which had accepted Jesus as the Messiah. Thousands had accepted him, including many ordained Jewish priests.

Our universal priesthood is rooted in Israel. Only the ordained Jewish priests could preside at the animal sacrifices, but all Jews shared in fundamental priesthood. For God had promised them that if they kept his covenant they would be "a kingdom of priests." Peter is applying this text to us in Christ.

The Jewish people believe that everyone born of Adam has the duty of helping God bring the human race to righteousness. As for themselves, they believe their special priesthood requires that they do this in accord with the Bible revelation given them. Similarly, we believe we have to carry out our priestly responsibilities in the light of Christ.

We can summarize by saying that, while only certain men are chosen by God and the Church for ordination to the ministerial priesthood and the diaconate, every Christian is baptized into the role of priestly worship and service. Like Christ our great High Priest, we are all sent to shed the light of God, and "go about doing good."

By tracing these roots of ours back into the Jewish faith, and even further back, into the origins of religion, we better understand ourselves. The Church developed and grew, just as each of us developed from a single cell. Only gradually did we develop into our complex bodies with all their organs and functions.

Similarly, the first reading shows the Church still developing, still coming into being. It is discovering its own needs, and the needs around it, and creating roles to fulfill those needs. It is just realizing that a gap has to be filled between the ministerial priesthood, and the priesthood of the people. The apostles have come to see that they are spreading themselves too thin when they try to minister to all the needs of the people. They explain that they must concentrate on praying and preaching the Gospel. And they invite the community to select men whom they will consecrate to certain corporal works of mercy. And so the diaconate was born.

From the primitive state in which we see it here, the permanent diaconate grew in numbers and function in the early Church, until it became an honored and esteemed priestly role.

Unhappily, it declined and ceased in later centuries. The Second Vatican Council saw the need for the diaconate, and called for its restoration. And now there are deacons in many parishes.

What are deacons? The Vatican Council tells us that they are part of the Church's governing structure. As in the days of Peter, they are appointed to duties of charity. The Council said that, though not ordained to ministerial priesthood, they are ordained to serve the people of God by assisting at the liturgy, by giving Holy Communion at Mass, and taking it to the sick; by presiding at prayer services and funerals, and performing many works of charity. Deacons serve in many parishes, but are most critically needed where there is a lack of ministerial priests.

The deacon is a special link between the hierarchy and the laity, the altar and the world, the spiritual and the corporal works of mercy. Deacons are often married men who work to support themselves and their families. They embed the Church's ministry more deeply in the world, in imitation of the Good Shepherd, who went out after the lost sheep.

A suitable candidate for the diaconate can be ordained whether he be single, married, or a widower, but after ordination he cannot marry, even if his wife dies.

Today's liturgy is a reminder to pray that the Christian priesthood may flower in all its forms, that is, in the priesthood of the laity, the deacon, and the ministerial priest.

We can best conclude by placing our shared priesthood in the context Jesus gives us in today's Gospel reading. The setting is the Last Supper, the night before he died. He promises to go ahead of us and prepare a place for us.

Now if Jesus went to prepare a place for us in the Father's house, our task in the meantime is to prepare ourselves to live in that house. How do we prepare except by clothing ourselves in the wedding garment of holiness and love? We gain in holiness by the priestly act of drawing close to God in prayer and worship. Ministerial priest, deacon, and all the people of God are, then, to cooperate in making our liturgy the holy, reverent, and saving action Christ intended it to be.

But there is no holiness without love, and there is no love without service. The literal meaning of the word *deacon* is *servant*. The service of deacons is the work of love. Let us honor deacons in the most honest way, the way of imitating their selfless service. The phrase, "Deacons restored," also means "Servants restored." Wouldn't it be marvelous if they inspire all of us to restore servanthood to the Church in the likeness of Christ? If we all serve one another in ways that will best prepare us for our Father's house, we will all be doing the work of Christ our great High Priest.

Ac 8:5-8, 14-17
1 P 3:15-18
Jn 14:15-21

GOD'S OWN TRUTH

Superconductors have caused a lot of excitement. If successfully developed, they will change our technology and way of life. From them will come everything from mighty midget motors to trains flying like magic carpets on invisible beds of magnetism. Superconductors carry current without resistance, so no energy is lost in heating wires.

By faith, we are conductors of God's truth, and by faithfulness, we are conductors of his love. Some believers are poor conductors. They have a lot of resistance, so that much of the love and truth they receive is lost. The saints are the superconductors of God's love and truth. Superconductors of God improve human life more than any technology.

On this Sunday before the Ascension, the Gospel promise of Jesus is that the Father will send us the Holy Spirit, the Spirit of Truth. Jesus calls him the Paraclete. In plain English, that means the Lawyer. He will help us penetrate to God's own truth, and defend us against the world's false charges. He knows all truth, and expresses it in a compelling way.

But I ask a question: Since God is love, why didn't Jesus call him the Spirit of Love? Wouldn't a lot more ears perk up? The reason is that Jesus is calling us to the truth about love. Everybody is eager for the rewards of love, but how many are ready for the hardships of defending the truth?

Truth is the necessary condition for true love. False lovers love without paying their dues to reality. They cut corners. Their love rests on an emotional cloud and not on the rock foundation of truth. Their love founders when the emotional cloud dissolves. Jesus sends the Holy Spirit to lead us to God, the One, the True and the Beautiful. When we build our love on truth, it endures because it is built on reality.

Jesus makes a shocking statement. He says the world cannot accept the Spirit of Truth. Strikingly, a Professor Allan Bloom wrote a book which says the same. In *The Closing of the American Mind*, he writes that American educators are open to every idea and opinion, but closed to the truth. If you have an opinion, however absurd, you are acceptable. If you claim to know the truth, you're cast out. The search for the truth about God and about moral conduct has been abandoned.

Why is that? One reason is obvious, and Dostoyevsky gave it. "Without God," he said, "everything is permitted." Isn't that what our culture wants — to have nothing condemned? Truth is adherence to reality, but how many want reality if it cramps their lifestyle?

Christ calls us to be superconductors of truth in a world which insulates itself against truth. Unless we accept the truths he taught, we cannot be his. "He who obeys the commandments he has from me," Jesus said, "is the one who loves me."

Truth is reality shining from the human mind. St. Paul urges us to be ready to cite the reasons for the true faith. If we know our faith, we can defend it well against its attackers and mockers. Unbelievers are the ones who are out of contact with the reality of God and his laws, and even his universe. We give evidence of this by pointing out that those who deny the moral law, and break it, are often destroyed body and soul. St. Francis Xavier, when a college student, held back from the corrupt life of his companions because he saw it destroying their bodies.

St. Paul himself closed his mind to the truth of Christ until knocked to the ground and asked, "Paul, why are you persecuting me?" Then he stopped denying the truth and became the Catholic teacher of the world. The great philosopher, St. Augustine, resisted the truth to follow wanton ways; when finally he yielded his mind to the obedience of faith, he became one of the Church's greatest teachers. St. Ignatius was more interested in soldiering than truth until felled by a cannon ball. His sick bed gave him time to think and pray and turn to Christ and his Church. Then he wrote, "What appears to me as white I will believe is black if the hierarchical Church so defines." And he added, "for it is by the same Spirit which gave the ten commandments that our Holy Mother Church is ruled and governed."

Our Blessed Mother was the first disciple of the truth of Jesus Christ. Pope John Paul II said that she is the model of the Church's faith. By believing and obeying, she brought forth God's Son, as by believing and obeying, the Church brings forth his brothers and sisters.

This sixth Sunday of Easter doesn't just prepare us for the Ascension of Jesus; it calls us to ponder how much we need the descent of his Holy Spirit of Truth to be the counselor of each of us in this very confused and misguided world. What good is freedom if we don't know the truth? A person lost in the desert may be free, but if he has no idea where to find food and drink, he is not free to save his life.

So, in the light of the Holy Spirit, we reflect that we are not really free until truth unlocks our chains of ignorance, false ideas, and false values. Only God's own truth does that. We take hold of his truth by believing his word. Then light is shed on the path we should freely take, and that is our true good. If we take it, it leads us to the true life given by the one God.

What does the Spirit teach us? To live the truth each day. To be honest with God and one another. To avoid lying to family or friends or anyone at all, for friendship is communication, and when it is falsified, love is falsified. To realize that lying corrupts the heart, as children seem to know, for it disconnects a person's tongue from reality, and his inside from his outside. That makes it hard for anyone to know and love him, even himself.

Can we do anything better than imitate the Virgin Mary in becoming superconductors of truth and love? Why imitate people

SUNDAY HOMILIES

we have seen rejoicing in their delusions until calamity struck? We are called to rejoice in the reality of truth. We celebrate the resurrection of the Son of God, receive his risen body in the Eucharist, and walk his way to everlasting life. That is the advice our Divine Lawyer, the Holy Spirit, is giving us.

"A" — Ascension Thursday

Ac 1:1-11
Ep 1:17-23
Mt 28:16-20

A NEW GAME PLAN FOR LIFE

Some years ago, men looked up into the heavens and gazed at the place where the race of human beings live. The gazers were the American astronauts who landed on the moon; the place in the heavens at which they gazed was the earth.

It is good to keep that event in mind as we reflect on the feast of the Ascension. What happened to Jesus in the Ascension, and what is its promise for us? The various readings and prayers for the Mass of the feast give us many clues to the answer.

In the first reading, we hear of Jesus ascending into the sky. The clouds cover him, and the disciples stand and stare at the point of his disappearance. If their feelings were words, we might hear something like this: "The Messiah has come; the Messiah has gone away; the Messiah will come again. In the meantime, our hearts sink; we feel abandoned."

Where has Jesus the Messiah gone? And what are we to do until he returns? As to that first question, we can say without hesitation that his physical ascension does not tell us where he has gone; but the opening prayer does. "God our Father," we pray, "may we follow him into the new creation." By his physical ascension, Jesus expressed his passage beyond time and space, into eternity, to dwell with the Father and share his glory.

What does Jesus' departure mean to us? Negatively, it means he will no longer be visibly present. His work on earth as mortal man is finished. But let us also see what it means positively.

Jesus spoke of its meaning for us. At the Last Supper he said, "I tell you the truth, it is better for you that I go. For if I do not go, the Advocate (the Holy Spirit) will not come to you. But if I go, I will send him to you." Thus, the departure of Jesus is the necessary prelude to Pentecost.

Let us lift our eyes, spiritually speaking, to the dwelling of God the Father. Imagine him recalling how he made human beings in his image and likeness, and saw that image soon corrupted by sin. After that it no longer radiated the truth that it was made in the image and likeness of its Creator.

And now, here is his Son, back from the Incarnation. Here at last, in all its glory, is the visible truth that man was made in God's image and likeness. From the body and soul of his risen Son shines the glorious likeness of God that he intended when he created human beings. And within Jesus is the grace to transform into his likeness all men and women who accept him in faith.

Who can imagine the outburst of divine love from that Father to his divine Son, and from the Sacred Heart of the Son to the Father? Is not that outburst of love the very outpouring of the Holy Spirit that the apostles will experience on Pentecost? The positive meaning of Jesus' ascension, then, is that his Holy Spirit can now descend and lead Jesus' followers into the new creation, and, one day, into glory with him.

But what are we to do until he returns? Certainly, we are not to stand staring into the sky, as the two men in white tell the disciples who witnessed the Ascension. We have work to do.

After death, we will be raised up and ascend to the Father. Until then we must live as a people destined for eternity. And if that is so, we need God's new game plan for human life.

Jesus expresses part of that game plan in today's Gospel: Make disciples of all the nations; baptize them, and teach them the way of Christ. We inherit from Christ the Father's own game plan. We, his body, are to complete his task. The work of Christians is to spread the Gospel.

How spread the Gospel? In the first reading, the apostles indicate they think it means restoring Israel's power now, making Israel a kind of heaven on earth. But that was not God's plan.

Do not some fall into a like trap today, trying to reduce the Church to an earthly kingdom of social do-gooders, when in fact the Church is a people on the march to a new creation?

Of course, admitting we are a new creation does not fully clarify our task. Our task is to spread the Gospel. Is it spread by preaching Christ's doctrine, or by engaging in social reform and social services? To put it another way, do we spread the Gospel by faith or by charity? By asking the question that way, we see the answer. We have to do both, or what we spread is not the Gospel! We can't spread the Gospel without believing and teaching what Jesus taught, but neither can we spread it without doing the deeds of love he did.

This issue is crucial. Some fail in charity in the name of faith; and some fail in faith in the name of charity. God's game plan cannot be stuffed into the tired old plan for an earthly paradise, nor can it be represented as pie in the sky which has no love for the living. Christ's Church is neither mere faith nor mere social charity.

St. Augustine sees this as the crucial issue. "This, in fact, is the difference between good men and bad," he writes. "The good men make use of the world in order to enjoy God, and the bad men would like to make use of God in order to enjoy the world — if, of course, they believe in God and his providence over man, and are not worse still, are not among the atheists."

Notice that the good as well as the bad use the earth, but for different purposes. We are not mere do-gooders. Jesus' ascension expands our horizons. We look beyond time, and act by the power of the new creation. The invisible Christ is within us, active in us, our very life. Today's postcommunion prayer puts its finger on the mystery. We say to the Father that, in the Eucharist, "we touch the divine life you give to the world." And we add, "Help us to follow Christ with love to eternal life where he is Lord forever and ever."

That is God's game plan, a plan that involves us in serving the whole world here and now, helping it realize to the full its potential. Human life is meant to be enriched by the wonders that love and human ingenuity can devise. This is a part of the work of charity; but its chief part is the duty of lovingly gathering all to us by faith. Then, together, as a great company, we will advance toward our resurrection and ascension in Christ Jesus.

"A" — Seventh Sunday of Easter   Ac 1:12-14
1 P 4:13-16
Jn 17:1-11

COMPANIONS OF GOD

A woman was told by her husband that he was suing for divorce. "Why?" she asked. He replied, "You have always been indifferent to my life. You never cared what I did or thought."

Let us imagine God the Father appearing to a Christian and saying, "We're close to breaking off." The person says in shock, "Why?" God responds, "You're indifferent to me. You never pray. You never seek my companionship in prayer. You don't love me. You never meditate on my teaching. You are indifferent to pleasing me. You have so little faith in me, you don't even ask for the earthly goods to which you are so attached."

If any of those charges can be leveled against us, we should be ashamed. How far from any such indifference to the Father Jesus was! In the Gospel reading at Mass on this Sunday we are privileged to overhear his prayer to the Father. His ardent prayer should fill us with desire to pray like him.

Jesus' words came not from memory, but from the heart. He prayed spontaneously. He talked to God aloud, in the presence of his apostles — and, through the Gospel, in our presence. This shared prayer is practiced today in the charismatic movement. To hear Jesus and one another pray guides us to better prayer.

The disciples may have prayed this way with the Mother of Jesus. We are told that, as they awaited Pentecost with her, they prayed constantly. Certainly, the Church has learned to pray to and with Our Lady. Her rosary is one of our most effective forms of prayer. With her, we go deep into the life of her divine Son.

Jesus prays to the Father about his concern for the work the Father entrusted to him, the work of revealing his truth and saving his people, and the work of glorifying the Father. By praying aloud, Jesus is saying to us, "You pray this way, too."

The first word of Jesus' prayer is "Father." In the Our Father, he taught us to begin the same way. In prayer, we can get locked into our own thoughts. Jesus' first word reminds us that it takes two to pray, God and self. This remains true even in the Mass. The core of all prayer is the twosome of God and oneself. Prayer is communication and communion with God. When we find Jesus at prayer in the Gospels, we often find him alone with God. He urged us, too, to pray alone with God.

We pray for four purposes: to adore God, to thank him, to find forgiveness, and to petition what we need. But what drama is hidden in those four purposes! Adoration is a love affair, a company-keeping with God himself. Prayer of petition is a child's confident presentation of needs to Father.

If we could enter Jesus when he prayed alone with God, we would find he prayed more with the heart than the mind. He used few words, as he told us to do. Prayer is more the love of God in our hearts than words on our lips. St. Augustine writes, "The constancy of your desire will be the ceaseless voice of your prayer, and that voice of your prayer will be silent only when your love ceases." Can we doubt that the great Reader of Hearts can hear our silent word of love for him? Let our lips and mind be silent often in prayer. Our hearts know how to speak to God.

Our prayer sometimes uses words, and sometimes does better without them. So we talk about two kinds of prayer, vocal prayer and mental prayer. Vocal prayer is either in a fixed form, like the Our Father, Hail Mary, and the Psalms; or it is made up on the spot. God's word teaches us how to pray. We should memorize many prayers, especially the Psalms. They help us pray in all moods and circumstances. They carry us high into prayer. They even launch us into the orbit of wordless prayer which we might rarely reach without them. They set our hearts on fire and we rest with God in the silent embrace of love.

In mental prayer, we begin by recalling Jesus' promise that he would dwell in us with the Father and the Holy Spirit. In God's presence, we slowly read a passage of Scripture, letting God speak to us instead of we to him. And so we ponder the mystery of God and man, of life and death, heaven and hell. Fires of insight flash out. Stirred by sorrow or joy, faith or hope, we address the Lord in silent words. All at once, our hearts burst into flame, and we cling speechlessly to God within us.

This wordless communion reminds us not to monopolize the conversation. God speaks wordlessly to us too. Unerringly, he moves our minds to his thoughts, and our hearts to his deep feelings, and our wills to the firm resolves he desires. Thus he guides our lives. To enhance this two-way communication, we should lace our prayer with silence, developing a listening heart. "Be still," Psalm 46 urges us, "and see that I am God."

Jesus' shared prayer is full of revelation, full of God's plan for our salvation. We will progress in prayer if we, too, make Scripture our subject of meditation. A rewarding mode of prayer is to read an event in the Gospels, close our eyes, imagine ourselves with the apostles, and live through the event as though present. It is like producing our own "life of Christ." But if it is to be prayerful, we have to be one of the actors too. We let Jesus take the role of director, speaking deep within us, giving us listening hearts, directing our actions, confirming our faithfulness, making us, like him, eager for noble deeds in accord with the Father's will.

Sometimes prayer is dark, unrewarding, dry, and seemingly worthless. That may be the best prayer of all. We give God our best efforts, and seem to get nothing in return, but we do not go away. We say, "Why have you forsaken me?" but we do not forsake prayer. And that is well, for no prayer is wasted, and this dark prayer may be the beginning of the best prayer of all. Mystical prayer begins with just such desolation and darkness.

In any case, this unrewarding prayer is a dying to self, a dying with Jesus. One day it will lead to resurrection with him, and ascension to the Father. That is the deepest purpose of every prayer life, to advance toward eternal life with the God of love.

"ABC" — Pentecost

Ac 2:1-11
1 Cor 12:3-7, 12-13
Jn 20:19-23

LOVERS' GUIDE

On a national news program some years ago, the announcer, speaking of Iran, exclaimed, "How do you deal with a people who believe they have a direct line to God?" Was he totally unaware that his Christian fellow citizens believe just that? Pentecost is the feast of our line to God, the Holy Spirit.

It is the feast of God as love. Imagine someone saying, "If love became visible, how would love look?" God's answer is to send love down in the form of tongues. There was first one tongue, but then it parted and settled on each one present. Is that not because the Holy Spirit is, as Jesus said, "the Spirit of truth"? Love is truth in action. That is why the Spirit also descended as a roaring wind. Like love, the wind can't be seen, but when it comes like a cyclone it sweeps all before it.

What Christian would not love to be present on the day the Spirit descended? And yet, on the eve of Pentecost, in 1987, the Holy Father prayed on TV with Christians around the globe. And in one sense, that was a greater event, for Pentecost foretold what that day expressed. Many tongues were heard, but all spoke in the one tongue of faith, in the one body of Christ.

The three Pentecost readings give three expressions of the Holy Spirit's action. He descends to strengthen the disciples on the day of Pentecost, and send them out as the missionary Church; he dwelt in the members of the early Church, as in us, imparting charisms, ministries, and missions; he makes the risen Jesus manifest to the joy of the apostles, and Jesus breathes on them the Holy Spirit, giving them the power to forgive sins in the Sacrament of Reconciliation.

Our Heavenly Father made his truth visible to us in his Son; his Son promised and then gave the Spirit to guide us in living the truth. The Holy Spirit inspired the prophets and the writing of the Scriptures. Now he illumines and guides the whole Church, collectively and individually.

When there was a faith-conflict in the early Church, the apostles expressed their faith in the Spirit's guidance in an unforgettable way. They called a council in Jerusalem, discussed the issues, and reached a decision. Their letter to Antioch said, "It is the decision of the Holy Spirit, and ours too, not to lay any burden on you beyond that which is strictly necessary." Here we have the apostles' express conviction that the Holy Spirit had guided their decision, and that they had a part in forming it.

It is our faith that Jesus promised Peter and his successors infallible guidance in solemnly defining dogmas, and ample guidance in working out all questions of faith and morals. As St. Irenaeus wrote in the early Church, "Where the Church is, there is the Spirit of God, and where the Spirit of God is, there is the Church."

We all received the Spirit at baptism, and were confirmed by him at Confirmation. He wants to instruct and guide each of us and fill us with the gifts of the children of God. Pope John Paul II said, "The Holy Spirit is active in enlightening the minds of the faithful with his truth, and in inflaming their hearts with his love." But, he added, the Holy Spirit uses the teaching arm of the Church to nourish us with the faithfully transmitted word of God. Only thus can our individual charisms mature and become productive.

The teaching arm of the Church must listen to its members, and we the members must respond to the decision of the teaching Church, as at its founding. We might recall here the announcer's troubled remark about Iran. Who can deny that not all who claim to be acting by the Spirit of God have in fact heard the Spirit?

Here is a guideline for tuning in to the Spirit: All that the Spirit does is marked by love. If we remember this, it helps us discern the Spirit's guidance from all the false and spurious impulses of self-ishness, and from all evil impulses.

True lovers want nothing less than the reality which they love. The Holy Spirit feels the same, and guides us to nothing less. He lives on in us as our companion in love, and counsels us always by the impulses of our hearts. He murmurs the same teachings to our hearts that he gave in the Gospels and gives in the Church.

Jesus said that the Holy Spirit will lead us to all truth. What is all truth but God himself, to whom the Church guides us? Are we troubled by the dissonance within the Church? The Holy Spirit calls us, on his feastday, to listen to him in our hearts, to listen to one another, but only wisely, and to give our best ear to the Holy Father and the whole teaching arm of the Church. If we all do this, the dissonance will clear away, and it will become evident that there is one flock, one Shepherd, and one Holy Spirit who unites us all.

Are we ready for those gruelling efforts to listen to the convic-tions of one another, to control our tempers, to speak kindly always, and to give to the Church our humble obedience of faith? This is what love costs. That great philosopher, Aristotle, observed that young people don't so much fall in love with one another; they fall in love with love. May the older generation, who are slower to open their hearts because they know the costs on the horizon, be converted today, be young in spirit, and fall in love with Love, the Holy Spirit.

It is fitting that this feast of the Holy Spirit, the lovers' guide, comes in the season of weddings. The Holy Spirit inspires all true love, and blesses all families with the gift of endless devotion, service, and forgiveness, if only they will open their hearts. Ordination gives the priest power to forgive in God's name, but love gives all of us the power to forgive in our own names, and that is a forgiveness we all need too.

So on this feast let us break the arrows of war, forget all hard feelings, mend all quarrels, and restore broken friendships. If we do that, who can doubt we are listening in to our direct line to heaven, for "Where charity and love abide, there God is ever found."

"A" — Trinity Sunday

Ex 34:4-6, 8-9
2 Cor 13:11-13
Jn 3:16-18

THE FAMILY GOD

A bright young college student, a science major, asked a priest about several doctrines of the faith. The priest referred to the words we say in the Creed each Sunday: "We believe in one Lord, Jesus Christ, the only Son of God, eternally begotten by the Father." The student asked what "begotten" means. The priest said it means "to be brought into being by a father," just as he was brought into being by his father. The priest further explained that when the word is used of God, it means that God really fathered a

Son from all eternity; and that, as the student was given human nature by his father, God's Son was given the divine nature by his Father, so that God's Son is God.

All this was a revelation to that student. He said the word "begotten" was an old-fashioned word he had never understood, and went on: "The next time you preach about the Trinity, you ought to explain that word, because there are many kids like me who don't understand it."

On the feast of the Holy Trinity we celebrate God as Father, Son and Holy Spirit. It is a feast of supreme beauty. It goes beyond all small matters and gets to the heart of religion. The essence of religion is intimacy between God and us. Intimacy means a relationship in which persons really get to know one another in a warm friendship, usually over a long time.

Only after many centuries did God's people come to know he had a Son. Adam and Eve were made as a family in God's image, and they knew God, but they didn't know God too was a family. God favored Moses with a great revelation of himself, and they became intimate friends. But it was not revealed to Moses that God is a family. That was reserved for the future, when God fulfilled his promise to send a Savior.

At last Archangel Gabriel was sent to the Virgin Mary in Nazareth. "The Holy Spirit will come upon you," he said to Mary, "and the power of the most High will overshadow you; hence the holy offspring to be born will be called the Son of God."

Here, to Mary, for the first time, the family God was revealed. The Father's Son was coming down to earth. By the power of the Holy Spirit, he would become Son of the Virgin Mother.

The Son of Mary did not come into existence when Mary conceived him; he had already existed from all eternity as Son of God. Through Mary, he also took a human nature, and became a man. And so we call Mary's Son the God-man.

It was not until God gave us his Son through Mary that God revealed he had a Son. The Father sent the Holy Spirit to bring her to conceive the Son in her womb. It was only through this giving of the Son through the power of the Holy Spirit that the Godhead was revealed.

The Father and Son have lived in love from all eternity. Their love is the Holy Spirit, the third Person of the Blessed Trinity. This is the mystery St. Paul celebrates when he writes, "The grace of our Lord Jesus Christ, and the love of God, and the fellowship of the Holy Spirit be with you all."

The Holy Trinity is a great mystery to us, the mystery of three Persons, three pure divine Spirits, so completely one that they are one God. Their sharing is so complete that the Father is God, the Son is God, and the Holy Spirit is God. Their union is so complete, there is only one God. They are one in being, and distinct only in their persons.

How can we understand so great a mystery? We cannot, but if we love greatly, we get a glimmer of understanding. Love yearns for union, and where love is perfect, union is perfect. That is all the answer we can have in this world, and those who do not know deep love have no answer at all.

God's overflowing love has poured out to us, and drawn us up into his divine family. We were baptized "in the name of the Father and of the Son and of the Holy Spirit." The Trinity did not become manifest at our baptism, but it became manifest for all of us when Jesus was baptized. He was visible in his human body, the Father was heard in the voice from heaven, and the Holy Spirit rested on the head of Jesus in the form of a loving dove.

By our baptismal rebirth, we were taken up into the Sonship of Jesus by becoming a member of his body, the Church. We became part of the family of the Holy Trinity. What we have become we will one day see in the glory of heaven.

We should feel very close to God. We have been taken up into the life of the most Blessed Trinity. Some people consider themselves close to God, but seem in fact to have only the external trappings of religion. How can we tell when we're really close? A sure sign is a sense of nothingness before God that comes from really knowing God. When a brilliant light comes close to our eyes, all else fades and we see only the light. When God comes close, all else fades, and we fall down in reverence, as Moses did. And with yearning love, we beg God to remain with his unworthy little creature, as did Moses.

Out of the closeness brought about by baptism, we yearn to honor God by believing in our new dignity and living it. We adore the Blessed Trinity not only by the way we pray, but by the way we live. Our divine Father is a practical Father. Even in passages of deepest sentiment and emotion, his Scriptures demand we cast out sin, and not fall into empty sentimentality. Even as St. Paul blesses us with the blessing of the Holy Trinity, he says, "Mend your ways."

Our God is a realist. He knows we cannot live with him as his children without growing holy as he is holy. Holiness inspires in us a spirit of adoration like that of Jesus. We have to realize we have tattered garments stained by sin. We wash them in tears of repentance; we mend our torn innocence with the spiritual needle and thread of prayer and good works; and so we become a little more presentable, covered with at least the garment of humility.

As part of the family of the Trinity, we should have often on our lips that most Catholic of prayers, "Glory be to the Father and to the Son and to the Holy Spirit."

"A" — Corpus Christi

Dt 8:2-3, 14-16
1 Cor 10:16-17
Jn 6:51-58

THE REAL PRESENCE

Years ago on Corpus Christi priests carried the Blessed Sacrament through the streets accompanied by worshipping throngs. In one parish the priest used to stop at appointed houses where altars waited. One ten-year-old boy filled with longing wanted to know why Jesus didn't stop at their home. "Ask the pastor," his mother replied. He did, and got his wish. "Jesus came to my house," he said proudly. "I think I'll go to work for him." And he did. He became a priest.

Heart and soul that boy held to the Real Presence of Jesus in the Eucharist. The Feast of Corpus Christi is meant to bring to all a heart-touched love for the great gift of Holy Communion and appreciation for the Holy Sacrifice of the Mass.

The Mass is a special kind of memorial which we can compare to a couple celebrating their wedding anniversary. They remember the day they wed, gaze into each others' eyes, and renew their love and their vows. In the Mass, Jesus comes to us and, in union with Calvary, offers his slain and risen body to the Father for our redemption. We join in the priestly offering and, at Communion, seal in love our baptismal union with him.

By offering his body and blood we experience the salvation he won for us and the peace of the kingdom — but only if our faith in the Real Presence is strong. By Real Presence, we mean that Jesus is present in the fullest sense of the word. He is as present as he was to Mary and Joseph in the stable at Bethlehem, and at their home in Nazareth. He is as present as he was to the apostles when he walked with them in Galilee, or sat with them at the Last Supper; as present as he was on the cross on Calvary; as present as when he visited the women and the apostles on the first Easter. He is as present as he is, body and blood, soul and divinity, to the Father in heaven. We can know it only by faith, but by love we can really possess his Real Presence in Communion.

We have many reasons for our faith in the Real Presence. It was foreshadowed when God fed the people of old with manna, which appeared each morning in the desert like bread from heaven.

It was promised by Jesus in Capernaum, as John's Gospel records. "I myself am the living bread come down from heaven," he said. Understanding he meant his real body and blood, many refused belief. Instead of backing down and saying, ''You take me in a wrong sense,'' Jesus turned to the Twelve and asked, ''Do you want to leave me too?'' He cannot back down. This is the way he is to give eternal life. He had just explained that by saying, ''Let me solemnly assure you, if you do not eat the flesh of the Son of Man and drink his blood, you have no life in you.''

Peter, no doubt, like the rest, stunned by his words, nevertheless cries out, ''Lord, to whom shall we go? You have the words of everlasting life.'' And Peter was there at the Last Supper when Jesus said plainly, ''Take and eat. This is my body.''

People of defective faith say the Eucharist is a mere symbol of Jesus' body. But how could he have been more plain, and how can a symbol give a share in eternal life? Can a symbol bring us to live in him and he in us, which Jesus says the Eucharist does? No, the truth is clear, and the faith of the Church is clear. We believe in the Real Presence on the authority of the Son of God.

St. Paul clearly taught the Real Presence when he said, ''Is not the cup of blessing we bless a share in the blood of Christ? And is not the bread we break a sharing in the body of Christ?'' All through our history faith in the Real Presence is evident. The second-century martyr, St. Ignatius of Antioch, urged Christians to ''partake of the one Eucharist, for one is the flesh of our Lord Jesus Christ, and one the cup to unite us with his blood.'' St. John Chrysostom said of the Eucharist, ''When you see it exposed, say to yourself: Thanks to this body, I am no longer dust and ashes, I am no more captive but a free man . . . This is the body he gave us to keep and eat, as a mark of his intense love.''

The Church long ago struggled to find a word to express what happens at the consecration of bread and wine into the body and blood of Christ. The Eastern Church used the Greek term, *metaousias,* ''change of being.'' By the thirteenth century, the Western Church called it *transubstantiation*. The Council of Trent said this word fittingly described ''that wonderful and extraordinary change of the whole substance of the bread into Christ's body and the whole substance of the wine into his blood, while the species of bread and wine remain.'' In plain English, the bread and wine look the same, but beneath their looks there is no longer any bread but the Bread of Life, Christ's body.

In answer to a resurgence of weak faith after Vatican II, Pope Paul VI reaffirmed the Real Presence. He said it is ''presence in the fullest sense. It is a substantial presence by which Christ, the God-man, is wholly and entirely present.''

The feast of Corpus Christi is a celebration and rejoicing in that Real Presence. At Mass, we re-present to the Father in an unbloody manner the body of Christ which he, our High Priest, sacrificed on Calvary. Through his Eucharistic presence, we enter into the feast of union with the Bread of Heaven. We make visits to the Blessed Sacrament to enjoy the comfort of Jesus' presence. We have benediction of the Blessed Sacrament to adore him present; and the Eucharist is kept ready to be rushed to us as Viaticum when we are dying and long for Jesus' companionship on the final leg of our journey to eternity.

The Friday following the Feast of Corpus Christi celebrates the Feast of the Sacred Heart of Jesus. The two feasts have a natural unity. By giving himself completely in the Eucharist, Jesus made it evident he wants to share his very heart with us. Where can we better enter his Heart than when he is before us in the Blessed Sacrament, or joined to us in Holy Communion? The fact is, Jesus gave the revelations of his Sacred Heart to St. Margaret Mary while she was adoring him in the Blessed Sacrament.

Thought of Jesus' Real Presence brings joy, joy that we possess Jesus even as we await him; and joy in the assurance that, if he gives himself to us even now, he will withhold nothing of himself and his life in the kingdom of our Father.

"ABC" — John the Baptist

Is 49:1-6
Ac 13:22-26
Lk 1:57-66, 80

IF JOHN THE BAPTIST WERE HERE

Are there any figures like John the Baptist in the world today? Who will carry on his work? From Advent to Trinity Sunday, the Church has relived the life of Jesus, from his descent into the world to his ascent to the Father. Now the liturgy makes it evident that John's work of making Jesus known must be carried on. Who will do it?

John will do it. In recalling his life of great service to God, we let John work in us still, by his memory and his prayers. We too must do what John did. The prophets before John could only promise the coming of the Savior; John made him known when he came. That is our work as well, even if our manner of doing it must be different. "If John lived my life," each of us should ask, "how would he use it to make Jesus known?"

A scrutiny of John's life will help us answer that question. John's origin involved a religious mystery. To his aged father, the Archangel Gabriel foretold his conception by his aged mother. We too, in our origin as Christians, share in religious mystery. By baptism we were born of God.

Despite his singular origin, John shares with us the important natural qualities of human life. Reflection on them can guide many to play their part in making Jesus known.

The question has been asked, "Who is more important, Pope John Paul II, or his mother?" Without his mother, we would have no John Paul II. And without Elizabeth, we would have no Baptist. The parenthood of these two women and their husbands prepared the way of the Lord. As God-fearing parents, they brought up their children to be what they became.

A careful study was done to answer the question, "How did good people get that way?" The gist of the findings came to this:

They got that way by the values they learned from their parents.

But goodness and right values alone don't produce outstanding men and women. They must develop characters marked by strength and confidence. A study of child rearing shows how these originate. When the child's chief provider, usually the mother, is caring and alert to babyhood needs, the child develops a sense of security. He feels free to explore and grow; his confidence in her helps him develop confidence in himself. And so when the time comes he confidently goes his way and fulfills his role. Is not this the image that John and his family convey?

"With the recognition that your love has led to God's creation of a new human being," one couple wrote, "everything else becomes slightly trivial." This is the picture Zechariah and Elizabeth give at the birth of John. Through John, they did their share in making the Savior known.

John continues to make him known. All who hear how he leaped for joy in his mother's womb are reminded of the humanity of the unborn child. By leaping for joy, John exposes the horror of ending a human life that is just beginning. By leaping at the presence of the unborn Child Jesus, John reminds us how human life has been sanctified all the more by the God who became man.

When a young man, John went off to the desert to fast and pray. We cannot make Jesus known unless we pray and learn to know him ourselves. So well did John come to know the mystery of Jesus that he professed he wasn't worthy to remove the Lord's sandals. Should we not know Jesus the God-man better than John, and grow more lowly still in his service?

So well did John come to know Jesus that the first time he pointed him out, he cried, "Behold the lamb of God who takes away the sin of the world!" As early as that John knew and hinted of the great mystery and terror of Calvary. Few Christians to this day grasp as well the mystery that suffering marks the work of salvation for Jesus and for us all. To serve others we must sacrifice, and to serve the truth we must endure persecution.

John compared Jesus to a bridegroom arriving at his wedding, told of his joy in the arrival, and concluded, "He must increase and I must decrease." Here is a model of zeal and lowliness for us all. John is one of the company of saints who can shame us if we are unproductive for Christ. He inspires us to do more.

His zeal brings to mind the great Apostle to the Indies, St. Francis Xavier. He was overwhelmed by the task of making Christ known to the teeming masses for whom no one seemed to care. "Again and again I have thought of going round the universities of Europe," he wrote, "and everywhere crying out like a madman, riveting the attention of those with more learning than charity, (and saying) 'What a tragedy: how many souls are being shut out of heaven and falling into hell, thanks to you!' "

We Catholics have always honored the saints. A Lutheran pastor urged us to hold to the practice. By their sacrifices, he said, they have given us the legacy of the faith; they remind us of our history, our tradition, and our continuity with Christ. To forget them is to impoverish our liturgy and deprive us of the Christian heroes and heroines who fill us with joy by their victories, and goad us on to our own.

No people possessed of love for country forget the great men and women who founded or served their nation. How much more should we honor those who gave us Christ and the Church? John the Baptist was the first to witness to Christ as the Savior of the world. He is a pillar of our faith, and a reminder that the task of making Christ known has been passed on to us. He became a "light to the nations," and so must we.

Each time, at Mass, when the words, "Behold the lamb of God," are pronounced, we hear the prophetic words of John teaching us still. And when we receive the Eucharist, we know that the divine Bridegroom has arrived in our souls, and John is glad to be forgotten. But let us not forget John's words, "He must increase, and I must decrease." And how will he increase if we do not carry on John's work of preparing the way of the Lord?

"ABC" — Solemnity of Saints Peter and Paul, Apostles   Ac 12:1-11
2 Tm 4:6-8, 17-18
Mt 16:13-19

PRAISING OUR FAITH'S FOUNDING FATHERS

Entertain for a moment this story that sheds light on our religious condition: War sweeps a country, scatters its people, and severs a teenager from his family. He inquires for them everywhere, but in vain. One day a stranger appears at his door with a letter. It reads, "Son, my dear friend, Peter, the bearer of this letter, will lead you to us. Trust him. With love, your Father." What joy when he is reunited with his family!

The war of sin has scattered us and separated us from God our Father. We have been sent the "letter" of the Bible, and given God's dear friend Peter to guide us home.

On the Feast of Saints Peter and Paul, we celebrate two believers who conquered their weakness, helped the Church to grow, shared the cup of the Lord's sufferings, and became friends of God. And so they are our friends as well. Celebrating their feast is a little like a combined holiday in honor of George Washington and Abraham Lincoln.

Through Peter and Paul, the Church first received the faith. Their feast is an invitation to enhance peace and unity in the Church. The world works for peace, but the work keeps foundering because there is no world-wide authority to enforce it. But in the Church God has given us the authority of Peter and his successors to bind us to unity and peace. To Peter Jesus said, "Whatever you declare bound on earth shall be bound in heaven." Peter and his successors have kept the faith intact for us all.

Christ founded his Church on Peter, a father in the Christian faith. Peter spread the faith among the Jewish faithful, and Paul carried it to the nations of the world. Ours is the Church that is one, holy, catholic, and apostolic.

Our Church is *one*. Paul said, "I have kept *the* faith." He received that one faith from Christ and his apostles.

Our Church is *holy* in its Lord, its Eucharistic worship, its saints, and its doctrine and moral teaching. It is so holy that at times members rebel against its teaching.

It is *catholic*, that is, universal, open to all peoples of all times and places.

Our Church is *apostolic*, the Church the apostles spread at the God-man's own command. This feast celebrates the apostolic nature of our Church. As the U.S. Constitution comes down to us from our founding fathers, faith in Jesus Christ comes to us from the apostles. Through them we are led to the one Lord, one faith, one baptism, one God and Father.

How beautifully Christ chose. Peter is very human, full of faith and enthusiasm for our Savior. By faith, he recognized Christ's eternal identity and said for us all, "You are the Christ, the Son of the living God." Peter received three special gifts: revelation from Jesus Christ, inspiration from the Holy Spirit, and the charism of infallibility. That charism was necessary to make his solemn pronouncements of faith worthy to be bound in heaven.

Peter followed Jesus in love, fell in weakness, and rose in tears and sorrow. Leading the Church as his office required, he lorded it over no one. He judged even St. Paul's doctrine, yet humbly accepted Paul's correction for not practicing what he preached. He is easy to love and imitate because we recognize in him our weakness, and find in him the faith and love we desire.

Peter's love overcame his weakness. Imprisoned in Rome's Mamertine dungeon for execution, he asked to be crucified upside down. Who is worthy to be crucified like the Lord? Peter never forgot he was the sinner who cried, "Depart from me, Lord, for I am a sinful man!"

Paul set the example we all wish to follow. "I have," he said toward the end, "kept the faith." He not only kept it, he gave it to the nations, "and became the teacher of the world."

Remembrance of Peter and Paul stirs our filial piety. The ancients of their day defined piety as love of God, father, and fatherland — the wellsprings of our existence. Who of us can pay enough gratitude to our Creator, parents, homeland, and Holy Mother the Church?

It is wrong to think we are passive observers in all this drama. When Peter professed his faith he spoke for us all, and we all live what he spoke. St. Augustine points out that Peter's name was taken by Jesus from *petra,* the common Greek word for rock, as our name, Christians, was taken from the word *Christus,* the Christ. Peter the rock was built on the God-man, the Rock of Ages, and we are pebbles built up on their foundation. The Church of God continues growing in us.

Though we received Christ's word through Peter and Paul, we receive his life directly from him in the Eucharist. And so we pray today, "Lord, renew the life of your Church with the power of this sacrament. May the breaking of the bread and the teaching of the apostles keep us united in love."

As we celebrate Peter and Paul, and recall that "Peter raised up the Church from the faithful flock of Israel," we look with reverence to our roots in the Jewish people. They were not all faithful, but no more are all Christians.

Have we joined ourselves to the Heart of Christ? Then that ancient people of God who prepared the way for him is dear to us. Since the Jewish Jesus is the Son of God, the Jewish Virgin Mary his Mother, Jewish Peter his chosen Pastor, and Jewish Paul our father in the faith, have we not an unpaid and unpayable debt to the Jewish people? Do we feel the impulse to share with them what we have from them? A beginning is to make room for that suffering people in our hearts.

Can we not hear Peter and Paul summoning us from heaven to thank God the Father for his Son, and the Son for his Church, and the apostles for their labors in handing on the faith? The best thanks we can give is so to live that when our time comes we can say, "I have kept the faith."

"A" — Thirteenth Sunday of the Year

2 K 4:8-11, 14-16
Rm 6:3-4, 8-11
Mt 10:37-42

IN THE BEGINNING, BAPTISM

Through the ages parents have gazed at their little boy or girl and wondered what kind of a man or woman he or she would become. They take it for granted that the child is destined to grow into a mature adult. Who would even think of doubting it? The history of all past generations makes it plain that within each child is concealed the principle of growth and destiny.

Within us there is another life with a similar principle and a higher destiny. It is the new life which began with faith and baptism. St. Paul teaches that through baptism we died to sin and were buried with Christ, so that as he was raised from the dead we too may have a new life.

Baptism produces on the level of invisible reality the things which the visible symbols of the sacrament place before our eyes. These visible realities are most evident in a baptism by immersion. The person goes bodily down into the water. Water can bring death, or it can originate life, as we all originated in a watery womb. In baptism, water and grace produce both death and life. With Christ dying on the cross, we drown our old, sinful nature; with Christ risen we come forth to a new life from the baptismal womb of our Mother the Church.

This new life is a new *kind* of life, the only life which can make heaven our destiny. Jesus said to Nicodemus, "I solemnly assure you, no one can see the reign of God unless he is begotten from above." And he added, "No one can enter into God's kingdom without being begotten of water and Spirit." St. John says plainly that those who believe in Christ were begotten by God.

Sometimes we hear that we were "adopted" by God, but it would be wrong to think that meant by a legal act. God adopted us by recreating us in the image of his divine Son. We are, by baptism, made into new creatures sharing Christ's divine nature. We are taken up into the life of Jesus.

St. John takes care that we make no mistake about this. He writes, "Dearly beloved, we are God's little children now; what we shall later be has not yet come to light. We know that when it comes to light, we shall be like him, for we shall see him as he is." In other words, just as that little boy and girl will become a grown man and woman, we will grow into maturity as God's sons and daughters, and only then will we see what we are.

Baptism is, then, a tremendous beginning, but only a beginning. It washes away all sin, creates a share in Christ's nature, and gives us the grace and the responsibility of living Christ's life. It prepares us to receive the other sacraments, especially the Eucharist. It makes us able to offer the Holy Sacrifice of the Mass with the priest, and gives us the strength to carry the cross of Christ in our life.

The new Rite of Christian Initiation of Adults puts much of this development before our eyes. The new Rite is really a return to the ancient rite of the early Church. It is an apprenticeship that goes on for months. Converts learn little by little to live the Christian life.

In the Easter Vigil Mass of Holy Saturday, the converts listen to the biblical readings summing it all up. They hear of the first creation, of the faith of Abraham in being ready to sacrifice his son, and of the delivery of the people of God to freedom through the waters of the Red Sea. Then they hear the readings which make it clear that these were only figures of the new creation, of the divine Son sacrificed for us, and of our being newly created as children of God. At this point they themselves are baptized and share in all they have heard.

All of this reminds the rest of us of what we are, of what covenant we have made with God, of what life we are to live. It is a life most of us began in infancy.

The tradition of baptizing infants comes from the apostles. The Church directs Catholics to have their children baptized as soon after birth as good sense permits. The child can then grow and mature in the life of nature and the life of grace together.

The ordinary minister of baptism is a bishop, priest, or deacon. But baptism is so important that in an emergency every Catholic has the responsibility of baptizing. The essential act is to pour water three times on the head of the one to be baptized, while saying the words, "I baptize you in the name of the Father and of the Son and of the Holy Spirit." Baptism is so urgent that even a non-believer can baptize in an emergency.

Baptism launches us on the great journey into life as God intends it to be, a journey from which we must never turn back. When Christopher Columbus set out across the Atlantic to find a new route to India, he traveled for some thirty days in three small ships. His frightened crew were so on the verge of mutiny that he pledged to turn back if they did not sight land in three days. On the morn of the third day they sighted one of the Bahamas, which he named San Salvador. If they had not, they would have turned back and been failures.

We too may feel at times like turning back. In strong language, our Lord commands us to follow him and never turn back. He makes no promise of turning back in three days if we do not sight what we want. He knows where we are going, and in three days he returned with resurrection life.

He charges us to love him more than father or mother, and to take up our cross and follow him. We were baptized into the cross. If we seek ourselves we find only ruin. If we seek him, we find out who we are.

Pope John Paul II points out that we were made in the image and likeness of the Holy Trinity. As the Father goes out of himself to the Son, and the Son to the Father, we find ourselves by going out of ourselves in love. Marriage is the natural form of this going out of self; faith is the divine form of going out of self, going out to

Christ into whom we were baptized. Our map is the map of faith, and the Church is our navigator, and the land to which the journey of baptism carries us is the homeland of God our Father.

"A" — Fourteenth Sunday of the Year

Zc 9:9-10
Rm 8:9, 11-13
Mt 11:25-30

THE SACRAMENT OF CHRIST'S COMPASSIONATE HEART

A non-Christian wrote a book on pain and suffering in which he states that God does not want us to be sick. There he is in harmony with St. Irenaeus, one of the ancient Fathers of the Church, who said that the glory of God is a human being fully alive. But our modern writer then adds that God can't make sickness go away. All he can do is inspire people to become doctors and nurses to help the sick.

Note what this writer is saying — that doctors can help, but God can't — that doctors have healing power God lacks! Such unbelief is a replay of the Sadducees, who didn't believe in the resurrection. We ought to answer such rank unbelief with Jesus' response to the Sadducees: "You are badly misled because you understand neither the Scriptures nor the power of God."

Lourdes shows to the world how wrong that writer is. Here is an eyewitness account of one young medical student who went to Lourdes to study firsthand any cures that might be reported. He saw a boy in a cart, twisted up with polio. His mother was crying out, "Holy Mary, help us." The bishop made the sign of the cross over the boy with the Blessed Sacrament. The boy rose from the cart. The crowd cried, "Miracle, miracle!"

The medical student examined the boy. "The Lord had truly

cured him," he writes. He then recalls how many of his professors on the Faculty of Medicine in Madrid lacked faith and ridiculed miracles, and adds, "But I had been an eyewitness of a true miracle worked by Jesus Christ in the Eucharist." That young student was Pedro Arrupe. He joined the Society of Jesus and became its Father General.

Jesus Christ healed in his day and heals in ours. He is the compassionate Lord. He gave us that sign of compassion called the Sacrament of the Sick. To administer it the priest lays his hands on a seriously sick person, anoints him with oil, and says, "May the Lord who frees you from sin save you and raise you up."

In the Gospels, Jesus calls us to him for healing. "Come to me," he says, "all you who are weary and find life burdensome, and I will refresh you." His Sacred Heart yearns to help us in our sinfulness, suffering, and sicknesses.

Jesus is at work in the Sacrament of the Sick, as he is in all seven sacraments. A sacrament is defined as a sensible sign instituted by Christ to give grace. The priest performs the action, but Christ produces the effect. St. Augustine makes this stand out when he speaks of baptism. He writes, "Those whom Judas baptized, Christ baptized." In every sacrament, Christ acts. In the Sacrament of the Sick, Christ acts on our bodies and souls.

How unwise it is to neglect to call for this sacrament when we need it! We should never use the excuse that the priest is too busy. He's not. The new Code of Canon Law says, "Pastors of souls and those who are close to the sick are to ensure that the sick are helped by this sacrament in good time."

Why doesn't God always heal the sick? Why does he let the sick suffer? Some people, like the writer I mentioned, seem to reason this way: "God is good. If he could heal the sick he would. So I guess he can't."

It's a bad guess. We Christians should know better. Through the cross of Christ God made suffering a healing remedy for sin and weakness. He made it a redemptive work for the salvation of all. A faith-filled Christian accepts suffering as his share in the redemptive work of Christ. Acceptance of God's will and our share in the work of redemption is more important than health.

For our part, we have a responsibility to stay as healthy as we can. The Rite for the Pastoral Care of the Sick says, "It is God's own plan that we should struggle against all sickness and carefully seek the blessings of good health so that we can fulfill our role in human society and the Church."

Our Lord loves us body and soul. When we call a physician to our bed, Christ wants us to call him too — the Divine Physician.

Even when Christ wants us to continue sharing his suffering in some illness, he helps us by the Sacrament of the Sick. The Council of Trent explained how: Through the anointing, the Holy Spirit takes away our sins and remnants of sin. He also consoles and strengthens us, and stirs our trust in God's mercy. He gives us power against temptation, and strength and sweetness in bearing our share in the cross of Christ. Finally, if it's really to our soul's advantage, he heals our bodies as well.

If we believe that one day God will raise our dead bodies, we surely believe that he can heal our sick bodies. So let's not neglect to call for his help through the Sacrament of the Sick. Call in the Divine Physician. He never makes a mistake.

We will lack confidence in our Divine Physician if we don't know him the way we know our dearest loved ones. He intends that we should. "Take my yoke upon your shoulders and learn from me," he says, "for I am gentle and humble of heart." This is the only place where the divine Son of God speaks of his human heart. "Enter my Heart," he is saying, "in prayer and love, and shared living." A privileged way of doing it is by the well-known Morning Offering, which consecrates our day to the Heart of Jesus.

With such turmoil in the Church since the Vatican II renewal, some of the most important things have been buried by the least important, and devotion to the Sacred Heart of Jesus is one of them. It suffered such a falling off that Pope Paul VI was asked about its status. He replied, "The Council was most concerned about the Church. The Church was born in the pierced Heart of Christ, and there it is nourished." Pope John Paul II called the Apostleship of Prayer, which promotes devotion to the Heart of Jesus, "a precious treasure from the Pope's heart and the Heart of Christ." He urged its spread everywhere.

Those who live in the Heart of Christ will know enough to use the Sacrament of the Sick when they need it. But they are the ones who are least likely to need it.

"A" — Fifteenth Sunday of the Year

Is 55:10-11
Rm 8:18-23
Mt 13:1-23

FAITH WE CAN DEPEND ON

Why, in recent years, have so many young people dropped out of the Church? If you asked a young dropout, "Why are you turning your back on God?" he or she is likely to look shocked, then say, "I'm not. I just don't need the Church and all that jazz."

What mindset lies behind that attitude? No doubt, a kind of "private enterprise" idea of religion. It's based on the notion that "I can deal directly with God, and get everything straight from him." But does God really takes the shortcut of fully revealing himself and his Christ and the way of salvation to every comer? If so, why not all be dropouts? But if not, the dropout is making a tragic mistake.

How does God reveal himself? The scriptural readings today remind us how — by making himself known in the whole course of history through word and deed, and finally through his Son, Jesus. Those words and deeds of God and his Son have come down to us through prophets and pastors and priests and all believers.

That's why we can't go it alone. It's not God's plan.

Of course, by reasoning, we can come to realize that there is a God, and that he rewards the good and punishes evildoers. But is that enough? It's not enough for God, and it's not enough for us who love him and want a surefire way to eternal life.

St. Paul says, "God in his wisdom made it impossible for men to know him by means of their own wisdom." To know God and his plan for our salvation we need the revelation as it's handed on. Revelation is God telling us about himself. Faith is believing him. Faith is to know God by God.

Now it's easy to find objectors who say, "I don't need the Church. Scripture is God's word — and that's enough!" It would be more accurate to say that it is half enough. The other half is the Church. The Church wrote the New Testament Scriptures by inspiration of the Holy Spirit, and is their only authentic interpreter. Jesus put his life's work and message in the care of Peter and the Church. The Church handed on the message by word of mouth and sacrament long before writing it down. And it never wrote everything down. Part of Christ's message lives on only in his body, the Church. The unwritten part is called tradition. Tradition is the Latin word for "handing on."

Only Scripture and tradition combined give us the Revelation in all its purity. And we have to go one step further. Only the teaching authority in the Church — the Pope and bishops — were promised the Holy Spirit's guidance to authoritatively interpret Scripture and tradition. We know how individuals interpret Scripture in contrary ways.

Further, only the teaching authority in the Church knew which were the real Scriptures. The Bible didn't fall complete from heaven. The Church put the Bible together from the true Scriptures, and rejected the false ones.

To know God's way, we need Scripture, tradition, and the teaching authority of the Church. These three are like the three legs of a tripod. With less, a tripod falls. With our faith resting on these three legs, we are in secure possession of what God wants us to know. These three legs are in the Church alone.

Jesus likens God's word to seeds planted in the soil of our hearts. The seed grows if we allow it to be fertilized with tradition, and tended by the gardeners in God's Church. If we don't allow it, our hearts are like the stony soil Jesus describes.

Jesus calls us to open our hearts to his divine teaching. It makes us more blessed than many a holy man and prophet of old who did not know Jesus. Catholics know Jesus by the light and love flooding in through Scripture, tradition, authoritative teaching, the sacraments, and one another. We are more blessed than kings. We are brothers and sisters of Jesus Christ, and sons and daughters of the King of kings.

We await the transformation of our bodies into the likeness of his glorified body, but we don't wait idly. We make the seed of his Revelation bring forth faith and fair deeds done. We want to be that good soil bringing forth thirty or sixty or a hundredfold. We don't aspire to go to eternal life alone, like the Church dropout. We grow a big crop of faith, to take thirty or sixty or a hundred others with us to our Father's home.

There is one place where we do have to go it alone, as the dropout wants to do. That place is private prayer. Private prayer is a most tender and intimate part of our Catholic relationship with God. In prayer, we commune and unite with God most privately and personally. The Church earnestly wants us to do that, for its purpose is not to put a distance between us and God, but to close and eliminate that distance. Prayer has many forms. Even when we worship together there should be moments when we are alone with God. The best of them is when we commune with the God-man after Holy Communion.

In that spirit of communion with God, let me close with a prayer which compares the Church to a sheepfold and a pasture in which Our Lord feeds us on his own body:

Our Savior from the Father's side, Lord of all the world, save us by your death and rising. Call us, Shepherd Jesus, to follow you and find salvation. Lead us to the pasture of life's food, and gather us into one flock in your own sheepfold. Guard us from the foe, and guide us to our Father's home. Amen.

"A" — Sixteenth Sunday of the Year

Ws 12:13, 16-19
Rm 8:26-27
Mt 13:24-43

THE BOOK

If you were marooned on a desert island, and could have one book, what would it be? Before choosing, listen to G. K. Chesterton's answer. He said, "A book on shipbuilding!"

A fond pastime of book lovers is to get hold of the latest list of best sellers, and pore over the selections. Such lists, however, almost always omit the best-selling book of all times, from which today's readings were taken — the Bible. The Bible is not static. New editions keep appearing and retailing in numbers which dwarf those of many a best seller. Updated translations like the New American Bible make it very readable; and fine footnotes like those in the Jerusalem Bible make it more understandable.

The tens of thousands of books which come out each year can be likened to the good and bad seed of today's parable. Some plant good ideas; some plant evil ones. The Bible plants the best seed of all, the seed of the word of God. As long as we're marooned on earth, we should have and cherish a good modern translation, and read it over and over, like a long letter from home.

We are fortunate that the Church has given us the new lectionary at Mass. It uses a lucid translation, and provides a wide selection of biblical readings.

To profit more from the Bible, every Catholic should know

something about the nature and content of the Bible, the manner of interpreting it, and the guidelines we need to do it.

Nature and Content of the Bible

The Bible is the inspired word of God, and so a prime source of our faith. The word *Bible* comes from the Greek, and means "The Books." And the Bible truly is a collection of books. Still, we talk of it in the singular as "The Book." Never do we call it simply "a book" because as God's word it is the Book of books.

The Bible is a very complex book, divided into the Old and New Testaments. The word *testament* means a solemn agreement or contract or covenant — here, the sacred covenant between God and his people. The Old Testament records God's revelation up to the coming of Christ. The New Testament records Christ's coming and the founding of his Church.

The Old Testament is a whole library of divine revelation. It contains books of the history of God's deeds, his law, and his revelation through the prophets. It encompasses books of divine teaching such as the Book of Wisdom from which today's beautiful first reading comes. It gives us that fountainhead of prayer, the Book of Psalms. It features that great mystical love story, the Song of Songs. On the surface, the Song of Songs is simply a passionate love story of a man and a woman. In its hidden mystical meaning, it is an allegory of the love between the divine Bridegroom and his people.

Interpretation of the Bible

This need to penetrate the deeper strata of meaning in the Bible brings us to what is called "literary forms." We're all familiar with the various literary forms in our ordinary books. A worthwhile novel employs fiction to teach us truths about human nature, but not the kind of "it happened this way" truths that we expect from a history book. A poem describing a woman's eyes as "two bright stars shining in blue loveliness" is not giving us a scientific text in astronomy. You see, then, that we're all acquainted with literary forms.

At times, though, it's not easy to tell the literary form of a writing. Pick up a hundred-year-old book of a man's life, and if it's not identified as fiction or biography, you may never know which it is. Similarly, if Jesus didn't tell us the story of the seeds and the weeds is a parable, we might think it actually happened — and it might indeed have happened. But whether it happened or not is unimportant. What's important is the story's power to bring home to us the battle between those who are for God and those who are against him.

Guidelines for Interpreting the Bible

In the Bible, it can be difficult to know what literary form is being used. The Bible was written in cultures very different from ours. And the inspired writers don't always tell us clearly whether they are speaking in parable or recounting history, or giving a mixture of both.

Let's take an example of the problem of literary forms in the Old Testament. The Book of Genesis tells us that God created the world and the whole universe in the course of six days, and that he rested on the seventh. Now, that God created the world is an article of faith; but did he create it in six days?

That great Father of the Church, St. Augustine, realized that we weren't to take the word "day" in its usual sense of 24 hours. He points out that a clue to a different meaning is given us where the account of creation speaks of three "days" *before the sun was even created!* He concludes that the days referred to here "are beyond the experience of us mortal earthbound men." So the account of creation can be understood in its details only by profound reflection and faith. The basic truth taught here is that God created man and beast and cosmos. He is the source of everything.

We see then that the awareness of literary forms in the Bible and the need to interpret them is not new. The rabbis of Jesus' time were aware of them, and so were the Fathers of the Church.

Christians who take everything literally in the Bible are called fundamentalists. Christians who too readily depart from the literal sense are toying with error and heresy. Even scriptural scholars agree that some interpretations offered by other scholars are just plain wrong.

The conclusion is that we need all the help we can get to understand the Bible rightly. We need scholars, historians and footnotes. We need the readings at Mass and the homilies of understanding preachers. Above all we need the guidance of the teaching Church and the light of the Holy Spirit. But all of this is too little if we don't read the Bible and pray over it, and apply it to our own lives. Think of the Bible as a long letter from our heavenly Father, containing love letters from the divine Bridegroom. If we love in return, we'll read it over and over.

"A" — Seventeenth Sunday of the Year

1 K 3:5, 7-12
Rm 8:28-30
Mt 13:44-52

THE LIVING GOSPEL

Hearts come in all qualities. Some are hard and insensitive; some are too flabby and sentimental to take on the shape of truth and true love. Today's readings summon us to seek a wise and understanding heart. Just such a heart was needed by Solomon to govern his people. Just such a heart is needed by each of us to govern himself as God wills.

Where shall we find wisdom of heart? In the field where God

invites us to dig it out like buried treasure. That field is the Bible. Christ is the pearl of great price found in the Bible. Since he is found in the Gospels, it is to that part of the Bible that we turn most, and turn now.

The Gospels are the heart of the New Testament, that is, the New Covenant. The Father has solemnly covenanted to make us his children by a marvelous rebirth in Jesus. And so at the Last Supper Jesus took the cup of wine and said, "This is my blood, the blood of the covenant, to be poured out in behalf of many for the forgiveness of sins." Jesus is our New Covenant with God. He is what the Gospels are all about.

To understand the fourfold Gospel of Matthew, Mark, Luke and John, we have to realize there is only one Gospel. The word *Gospel* means "the Good News," and Jesus *is* the Good News. His birth, his preaching, his power, his saving life, death and resurrection and his Church are what is proclaimed in the Good News.

The apostles went forth to preach the Gospel of Jesus. At first, the word *Gospel* did not mean a piece of writing, for it hadn't yet been written. It meant the passing on of the Good News by word of mouth. We call that the oral tradition.

Perhaps surprisingly, the oral tradition is still crucial today, for some of what Jesus said and did was never written down. It was simply passed by word and example from generation to generation in the Church. The Second Vatican Council said that the apostolic word of mouth is to be preserved to the end of time by a continuous succession of preachers. Jesus Christ whom I proclaim today *is* the Gospel. I preach Jesus, the hidden treasure of God concealed through the ages, foretold by the prophets, coming forth from Mary's womb, and revealed to the nations. Jesus is both Source and Subject of the Gospel. He *is* the Good News.

Now let us try to picture how the spoken Gospel came to be written. Within 30 years of the resurrection, the Gospel had been preached in much of the known world. By now, some of the disciples who had lived with Jesus had died, and the rest were in great demand. How could they possibly satisfy the thousands who hungered to hear them tell of what they had seen and heard? So certain apostles and their followers were inspired by the Holy Spirit to write what they knew. There is evidence that the first writings were not the complete Gospels we know, but brief accounts of the Lord's passion, death and resurrection.

The Gospel of Mark is generally accepted as the first-written of the four Gospels. It was composed between 30 and 40 years after the resurrection. Mark was a disciple of Peter, so it is probable that Mark's Gospel is in large part a kind of "Gospel of Peter." Mark's is the Gospel of the discovery of Jesus' identity. At first, the Jesus of Mark's Gospel is seen only as a prophet full of the human qualities we love. But as the Gospel goes on, discoveries are made. This Jesus has great powers. He works miracle after miracle. He forgives sins. He fulfills prophecies. Then the light dawns and Peter cries, "You are the Messiah!" Later, when Jesus is before the Jewish Court, the most stunning disclosure of all is made — Jesus is the Son of God.

The Gospel of Matthew was written at least 40 years after the resurrection. He shows that Jesus is the fulfillment of the Old Testament prophecies. He is the promised Messiah. Christians must go out with zeal to make him known to the nations.

Luke the physician wrote his Gospel about 45 years after the resurrection. Not having known Jesus, he went for his sources to those who did. It may be that he spoke with the Mother of Jesus, and that his infancy narratives are in part a kind of "Gospel of Mary." Luke shows that Jesus was the Savior of all people, but especially of the poor and oppressed. He points out how Christians too are oppressed. They respond by loving even their enemies. They speak the prophetic word and proclaim the call to justice with the power of the Holy Spirit.

The fourth Gospel was written by the Apostle John, though many scholars think others had a hand in its final form, with John as the authority behind it. Tradition says John lived to a great age, and in fact his Gospel was composed 60 or 70 years after the resurrection. John's Gospel is notable for its tremendous emphasis on the divinity of Christ. He tells us much about the Savior's inner self and transcendent mystery. John's Gospel soars up to the inner life and mystery of the Trinity.

Now a word about the final Gospel to be written. The Gospel did not begin with books but with people. It began with the God-man, and continued in the men and women who preached him. The final Gospel for each Christian is the one each of us writes with his life. The way we live is a true or false Gospel of Jesus.

The four Gospels are inspired and error-free through the power of God at work in the authors. His power is at work in us too, to make our lives authentic versions of the Gospel.

To live the Gospel, we must steep ourselves in it like cloth steeped in dye. Our Catholic tradition tells us this is done by a three-phased activity. We take the Gospels and read them, meditate on them, and pray over them. By reading them slowly, and preferably aloud, we have already begun our meditation. The slower we read, the better, for we have to "chew" the Gospels as we chew food. The moment we see an application to our lives, we pause and ask the Lord's help, so now we are praying.

If we do this for weeks and years, and live what we learn, we gradually become authentic versions of the Good News. We become living Gospels of Jesus Christ.

"A" — Eighteenth Sunday of the Year

Is 55:1-3
Rm 8:35-37, 39
Mt 14:13-21

HUNGER NO MORE

"A loaf of bread, a jug of wine and thou," writes the poet-lover, Omar Khayyam, as though that said everything. In today's

Gospel, Jesus, too, expresses his desire for his beloved people to share bread in his company. "There is no need for them to go away," he declares. It didn't matter that there was not enough bread. Wine had run out at Cana, and he provided it. Now he would do the same with bread.

Pilgrims who travel to the Sea of Galilee visit with reverence the ruins of an ancient church near Capernaum which commemorates this multiplication of the loaves. You can see in the stone floor near the altar a beautiful mosaic representing a basket of loaves and fish. The pilgrim Egeria who traveled there at the end of the fifth century reported seeing the church. But invaders of the seventh century destroyed all but the flooring.

We can appreciate Jesus' tender love in this event only if we enter into his heart. He had just been told that his beloved cousin and brave herald John had been murdered. His heart felt in need of healing, and he tried to go off alone with the apostles. But the people followed, so he forgot his wounds and healed theirs. He labored in teaching, the day passed, hunger came, and he fed the people.

Jesus feeds people still, with the hearts and hands of his members. A seminarian visiting a TB clinic was told by a poor sick man there that when he was down and out on the streets he could always get a little help at a Catholic rectory.

Our first impulse is not always to help. When Jesus told the apostles to feed the crowd with the little available, they must have felt their own empty stomachs shrinking further. They objected that there wasn't enough, but were overridden.

In God's providence, there is always enough. God provides more than enough, but doesn't distribute it evenly. It is for us who have more than we need to share with those who have less than they need. We never have to impoverish ourselves; we only have to give so that no one goes without. We all recognize this as the Christian message taught from the beginning.

St. Caesarius of Arles said in a homily, "What kind of people are we? When God gives, we wish to receive, but when he begs, we refuse to give. Remember, it was Christ who said, 'I was hungry and you gave me nothing to eat.' '' God feeds us in many ways, and we his followers help him feed others in those ways.

There is no question that the hands of Christ extended in his members have given loaves by the millions, and continue to do so. We need only be sure that ours are among those helping hands.

We now go on to reflect that more than bodily hungers are involved in these events. When Jesus fed his followers' bodies, he fed their hearts even better by the love of his heart, and we can be sure they didn't fail to understand that. The word of God always implies more than bodily hunger for if man lives by bread, he does not live by bread alone. The Lord knows the hungers he created in us for our bodily needs, but above all for love, peace, union with him and one another, and everlasting life. He yearns to fill them all in accord with our state of life.

What would you think if a priest who served you should look at you and say, "My people are concerned for nothing but material things"? Wouldn't you be offended? Surely, God would. He made you and he knows your heart is restless until it rests in him.

No doubt, any of us can stray from our real hungers to what can only be called trivial hungers by comparison. Charles Francis Adams wrote, "Failure seems to be regarded as the one unpardonable crime, success as the all-redeeming virtue, the acquisition of wealth as the single worthy aim of life." That has the sound of something written yesterday, but it was penned over a century ago. The renowned artist, Salvador Dali, was a self-professed victim of such wrongful hungers. "I think," he once said, "that any means are justified to achieve celebrity."

Compare his appalling attitude with that of St. Ignatius. He said that, since we were made for God, we shouldn't care whether we have a long or short life, riches or poverty, sickness or health. We should put ourselves in God's hands, and look only to what best returns his love.

We know St. Paul was like that. St. John Chrysostom says of him that as long as he had Christ's love, "he thought of himself as possessing life, the world, the angels, present and future, the kingdom, the promises, and countless blessings." Death and pain he took as child's play if only he pleased Christ. And he combined all this with such devotion for those he served that when he parted from them he shed tears like a tender-hearted old grandfather overcome with love.

The Lord who fed the hungry desires to fulfill our holy and our best desires. He began when he gave us new life in the waters of baptism. In Holy Communion he feeds us with the bread and wine of his body and blood and gives us the gift of resurrection, of life through his risen life. Without payment, God gives us the bread of love, peace, joy, innocence, and abounding life.

We should never betray our holiest desires. When people feel a desire for the Eucharist, they should say, "Lord, I love you, and I'm going to eat your banquet with you today, even though it's not Sunday." Of course, sometimes it would be wrong. People have many responsibilities. St. Francis de Sales said that true devotion never interferes with anything, but only perfects everything. He said devotion that impedes our duties is false devotion. He knew that married people must have more concern about increasing their income than monks do. But if one feels a yearning for the Eucharist and can't attend Mass, he can at least express his desire to Jesus in a prayer of spiritual communion.

As we reflect on how Jesus fed his people miraculously, let us conclude by recalling that he is going to feed us even more marvelously today. One church has in the memorial book commemorating its opening the words of Jesus, "Where is the room where I am to celebrate the Passover?" Hopefully we will answer in our hearts, "This is it, Lord, and I'm very hungry."

HELP BEYOND HOPE

Human wisdom says, "There are no atheists in a foxhole." Are there any more in a bad storm at sea? Two men fishing off Key Largo were capsized by massive waves. They climbed on the keel again and again, only to be swept off until they could climb no more. Thinking God their only chance, they prayed. A yellow boat appeared. They were saved.

The apostles were in a boat on the Sea of Galilee. That Sea lies in a deep cleft of the earth, some 700 feet below sea level. It is a heart-shaped lake, thirteen miles long, with a breadth of over eight miles at its widest, and a depth of over 200 feet at its deepest. A lot of water lay under that rocking boat, and those anxious men must have sensed every foot of it.

But there are questions the events in today's Gospel should raise in our minds. Ours is not a religion of empty show. Why did Jesus walk on water? And why should Peter ask to walk on water, and in fact do so? To answer these questions, we have to get deep into what was happening. But since the other readings also contribute to the answer, we look at them as well.

All three readings describe God coming to the help of his people in trouble.

Elijah has run from the murderous hatred of his idol-worshipping queen. He has almost despaired of God's help. Terrible winds, earthquake and fire came, but only when a gentle wind arrived did the prophet bow down. God had arrived, and God spoke with him.

St. Paul is in trouble. He so loves his people that he would sacrifice his own salvation for theirs, but they are battling him. He can only put matters in God's hands, and wait, for God has revealed to him that one day he will draw his people to Christ. We can pause here for just a moment to reflect. Today in the Church there is a crisis of doctrine and a battle of faith. Paul teaches us to stand firm in the faith, but never to cease loving the brethren. To do otherwise would be to deny the primacy of charity, the greatest truth of all.

The apostles are in trouble, but to understand what happens, we must ask and answer the questions I posed.

Why did Jesus walk on water? And why did Peter ask to do the same?

To understand Jesus' action, we must realize how little time he had to reveal his identity to his apostles, and confirm them in faith before the scandal of the cross. Not only that, but soon he was to promise the Eucharist, which would try their faith. And so he helped them by a sequence of events.

First, as we recalled in last Sunday's Gospel, he made a little bread do what it cannot, that is, feed a crowd. Now he makes a body go where it cannot, that is, walk on the surface of water. Seeing these things, they were helped to believe that he can make his risen body go where bodies cannot go, into a piece of bread, and do what other bodies cannot do, feed the whole Church with resurrection life.

Let us add that Jesus walked on the lake to go to his apostles in trouble; but why did Peter ask to walk on water? We can make an educated guess by putting ourselves into his mental framework. He had been with Jesus for some months, and accepted him as the Messiah. If there was one thing he knew, it was that Jesus was a man like himself, not one of those angels who had appeared to his forefathers. And now everything is cast into doubt! Jesus is walking on water like an angel! No! He isn't an angel, and I'll prove it! Lord, call me over the water to you! And Peter walked on water — until he doubted, and sank, and was rescued.

Understanding this is too little unless we understand that

Jesus is with us, too, in help beyond hope. In our storms he is present. It is then we must remember that the real marvel is not that Jesus walked on water, but that Peter walked on water. Sometimes such troubles come into our lives that we feel we have to walk on water. Well, then, let's walk on water! We need only ask God to bear us up on our sea of troubles, as Peter did.

The storms are many. We may be lashed by a stormy marriage, straying children, an impossibly demanding vocation, a walking into the future with some dread disease. Or there may be an overwhelming history that grips us, a history of drugs or drink or the iron shackles of a sin that claims us again and again.

God's help beyond hope is there for us. If we call out with the faith of Peter, Christ will hear us too. And if we start walking, and sink again, he will be there to grab hold of us too, perhaps not at once, but before it's too late.

Some people react to the law of God and the teaching of the Church as though they are being asked to walk on water. They consider the demands unjust. The Psalmist knows that the call of truth can look unkind, and the demands of justice provoke unrest. But he also knows that when God's grace floods in on us, "kindness and truth shall meet; justice and peace shall kiss."

That grace will flood in on us if we, like Elijah, learn how to listen to the Lord. His voice is not present in the pagan storms of immoral demands made all around us, but in the gentle wind of his Holy Spirit entering our hearts and our consciences.

In all the troubles told of in today's readings, God comes and helps, and that makes us hope in his help too. We can bolster our confidence further by reflecting on the truth in the opening prayer: "Almighty and ever-living God, your Spirit made us your children, confident to call you Father." What good father does not come to the rescue when his little children cry out in need? And as to his being our Father, Jesus taught us that compared with our heavenly Father, our earthly father isn't even worthy of the name. No more can our earthly father's strength be compared with God's.

So we can be sure that help beyond all hope is waiting for us if we learn how to pray and call with faith on our Father.

And one more help is handed us in the rescue at sea. If Jesus was preparing his disciples for the reality of the Eucharist, he was preparing us too. Just as he walked on the water, he will "walk into" us today in Holy Communion. We would do well to greet him with the words of his first disciples: "Beyond doubt, you are the Son of God."

"ABC" — The Assumption

Rv 11:19; 12:1-6, 10
1 Cor 15:20-26
Lk 1:39-56

MARY THE MODEL CHRISTIAN

Good salesmen carry with them the best sample of their products. Artists showing their works hang their finest paintings. Christ our Lord, who longs to attract us to his salvation, sets his Mother before us as the most sublime expression of his redemptive work. He is the perfect Redeemer, she the perfectly redeemed one.

Still we would be turned from the truth if we pictured Mary as passively receiving gift after gift without having to struggle and labor. Just as we do lifelong battle to live by the grace given us, so did she. As Christ himself had to labor and be tempted, so too did Mary — though, like him, without sinning.

Mary is the model Christian because she is the model of faithfulness, of discipleship, and of apostleship.

Mary is the model of faithfulness. Never did she fail to hold God as the beloved of her soul, and see heaven as her final goal. She was assumed into heaven as the reward of her faithful life.

We rarely think of Mary before the Annunciation, but that's an omission. From childhood she was a faithful member of the

Jewish people. Only after years of girlhood fidelity was she summoned to be the Mother of the Messiah whom she was so faithfully awaiting. When, at the Annunciation, she said, "Be it done to me according to your word," she was only mirroring what she had always said.

She had always prayed. Now she had to pray more than ever, to grow in faith and understanding. She prayed over how God revealed her chosen motherhood to the infant John the Baptist, to Elizabeth, to the Jewish shepherds, and to the Gentile wise men. Throughout her life she "treasured all these things and reflected on them in her heart." She is the model of prayer. Without prayer, there is no faithfulness.

Undoubtedly, Mary is a model of *all* the virtues. She is a model of mothers and a model of virgins. One cannot help wonder at the prophetic meaning here. In this new age, both these roles strengthen and console marital couples who practice natural family planning, as they will understand.

Who cannot profit by reflecting on her maternal role? She reared Jesus at her knee. Nazareth, as Pope Paul VI said, is where we learn about family life, and learn silence, not noise, conflict and claims; we learn work and discipline and their redeeming values. Mary adjusted herself, sometimes in pain, as we all must, to the mystery of Christ's ways, as when he remained in the Temple at twelve.

Mary is the model of discipleship. When, during his public life, resistance to him was mounting, she went to him to affirm her loyalty and offer her aid.

When Jesus said, "He who does the will of my Father in heaven is brother and sister and mother to me," she rejoiced, for this gave her a second title to being called his mother. It was by doing his will that she had conceived him. And she knew that believing itself is nothing but obeying with the mind.

None was a more loyal disciple and comrade of Christ than she. She embraced his words, "Anyone who does not take up his cross and follow me cannot be my disciple.'' When others ran, she stood loyally at his nailed feet. How truly Simeon had prophesied to her, ''You yourself shall be pierced by a sword.''

Mary is the model of apostleship. She not only followed Christ but labored with him. She taught others to obey as well. At the wedding in Cana she said, ''Do whatever he tells you.'' She realized that intercessory prayer was a necessary part of the apostolate, and she intercedes for us still.

Her motherly role, first for her Son, and then for his body the Church, is the model of all apostolic work. The Second Vatican Council said, ''The Virgin Mary in her own life lived an example of that maternal love by which all should be fittingly animated who cooperate in the apostolic mission of the Church on behalf of the rebirth of men.''

Pope John Paul II, in his Apostolic Letter on the Dignity of Women, emphasizes this model apostolic role of Mary. Recalling the fact that Christ is the divine bridegroom of the Church, he states that ''all human beings — both men and women — are called through the Church to be the 'bride' of Christ.'' He adds that, ''In this way, 'being the bride,' and thus the feminine element, becomes a symbol of all that is 'human,' according to the words of Paul: 'There is neither male nor female; for you are all one in Christ Jesus.' ''

The Pope goes on to point out that before the fact of the mighty works of God, cooperation with God is such ''that St. Paul, as a man, feels the need to refer to what is essentially feminine in order to express the truth about his own apostolic service''; and so Paul described his converts as ''my little children, with whom I am in travail.''

So Mary is the perfect model of the call to apostolic service. She did more than any of us to help Christ bring his Mystical Body into being. St. Augustine states that she ''is clearly the mother of the members of Christ . . . since she cooperated out of love so that there might be born in the Church the members of Christ the Head.''

Mary is also our intercessor in life and in death. What loving mother with her power as mediatrix of grace would not plead for her children, guide them, and see that at the hour of their death they come trooping home to God their heavenly Father? What mother could do this more lovingly than Mary?

In return we owe her true devotion. True devotion embraces her as both Mother and Model. Vatican II says that "true devotion . . . proceeds from true faith, by which we are led to know the excellence of the Mother of God, and are moved to a filial love toward our mother and to the imitation of her virtues."

To give our Mother a gift on this feast of her birth into heaven, let's promise her we will imitate her in praying, obeying and serving until we too follow her Son into eternal life.

"A" — Twentieth Sunday of the Year

Is 56:1, 6-7
Rm 11:13-15, 29-32
Mt 15:21-28

CALLING ALL NATIONS!
CALLING ALL NATIONS!

The Tyre and Sidon of today's Gospel are in modern Lebanon, that place of untold terrorism and suffering in our time. If, as Jesus says, his mission was to Israel, why did he go to that foreign nation? Perhaps he went to Jews settled there.

More likely, he went for another reason. Did you ever feel that everything you worked and lived for was falling down around your shoulders? That you had to get away for a while? Such may have been the mood of Jesus and his disciples. Jesus knew from the beginning that he would be rejected and crucified; but now he and his disciples were experiencing the rejection. That, together with their exhausting labors, must have left them near to collapse. They had to get away and get a rest. That may be why the apostles were so annoyed by this pagan woman. Somehow, she had sniffed out the identity of Jesus, and ruined their vacation.

The vast and sweeping panorama presented to us by today's readings can be summarized in three statements: First, God planned the salvation of all peoples long ago; the Jewish prophets foretold it, and the Jewish people prayed for it. Second, God's firstborn people, the Jews, remain chosen, and will respond to Christ one day. Third, Jesus' mission was to the Jews, and through them to us, and through us to them.

First, then, God planned of old to invite all peoples to join his Chosen People, the Jews. Today's readings and many others in the Bible make this evident. "My house shall be called a house of prayer for all peoples," says God in the first reading. The Jewish people were God's platoon of salvation marching into the world.

At Auschwitz, in 1979, Pope John Paul II spoke to Jews of "the mysterious link which brings us close together, in Abraham and through Abraham, in God who chose Israel and brought forth the Church from Israel." There is God's mystery, which we ponder today. To see how deep it goes, know that an earlier Pope, Pius XI, said, "Spiritually, we are Semites."

Secondly, God's firstborn people remain chosen, and will respond to Christ one day. Paul makes this too plain to deny when he says, "God's gifts and his call are irrevocable." Once God calls you and me and the Jews and anyone else, he calls on and on no matter how long we reject him, for his love is everlasting.

Paul also points to another mystery, the mystery that the Jewish rejection of Christ actually opened the way for our salvation. Paul learned this by experience. When he made it plain to non-Jews that most Jews had rejected Christ, somehow that attracted them the more, perhaps out of compassion for Jesus. But also, Paul tells us that he worked all the harder for the non-Jews to stir his brother Jews to wake up to what they were missing. If the Jews had accepted Christ, Paul might have taken it easy, and we'd never have the great Apostle to the Gentiles.

Paul makes a radiant prophecy. He says that if we benefited by the disobedience of the Jews, we will benefit even more by their turning to Jesus. And he says that benefit will be "nothing less than life from the dead!" What can that mean but the Second Coming and the general resurrection?

Thirdly, Jesus' mission was to the Jews, and through them to us, and now, through us to them. Jesus offered the Jewish people the chance to be his faithful followers, and the kernel of his kingdom. He owed this to them as the Chosen People, even though by divine knowledge he knew they would reject him. But we talk too easily and too wrongly about their rejecting him. Not all rejected him. The early Church was made up of the Jews who accepted him. These Jewish Christians made so many converts that the non-Jews eventually took control. We should never forget that we owe our salvation to the faithful Jews.

Even though Jesus was sent to the Jews, he rewarded that fierce faith of the pagan woman. But we should notice how he put her to a grievous test first. "It is not right," he said, "to take the food of sons and daughters and throw it to the dogs." At that point, how many of us would have stalked off, highly indignant, swearing that this carpenter was no prophet?

Christ is teaching all of us non-Jews a severe lesson here, if we can take it in. The lesson is that we non-Jews are not the first chosen, and had best not forget it, and not lose our reverence for those who are. This should teach us that for love of the Jews who gave us Jesus, we owe a special love to all their countrymen. Persecution of the Jews is one of the horrors of history. It is unjust, since the relative handful of Jews who plotted Jesus' death are long since dead themselves. It is a betrayal of Christ, since he charged us to love everyone, even our enemies. Pope John Paul II said, "No valid theological justification could ever be found for acts of discrimination or persecution against Jews. In fact, such acts must be held to be sinful.''

Through the ages to the coming of Christ, the Jews prayed for us, as the Psalms make clear. At his coming, the Jews who accepted him carried him to the world, as the New Testament makes clear. What can we do in return?

Whatever we do, we must do it with love, and do it discreetly. The Jews are, in a sense, our elder brothers, as Pope John Paul II said to them in Rome. It's hard to preach to an elder brother, as we ought to know. We can be humbled by our origin from them, sobered by our own trials, and kind to those yet to be called as we were.

We can pray as earnestly for them as their ancestors prayed for us. We can be always friendly and brotherly. We can become real Christians. If we live a life of deep faith in Christ, and of goodness and holiness and kindness and love, some Jewish people will be drawn to Christ, as Paul said. In this way, we can make a return for the Savior the Chosen People have given us.

And today, on receiving Holy Communion, we can be mindful of the Jewish Jesus, born of his Jewish Mother Mary, and consult his wishes about what we are to do that his people and all peoples may come to him, the Savior of the world.

''A'' — Twenty-first Sunday of the Year   Is 22:15, 19-23
                                                           Rm 11:33-36
                                                           Mt 16:13-20

CHRIST, PETER AND THE POPE

In a novel of some years ago called *The Priest,* the protagonist, Fr. Frank, suffers a vocation crisis. He reflects on his problem in these words: ''Dear God, he did not want to be a judge,

. . . the bureau of standards of the acts of mankind. Was it distaste for that burden, more than the itch of the flesh, which accounted for men leaving the priesthood?'' How would you advise this struggling priest? And more profoundly, how do today's readings answer and advise him?

The readings of the last two Sundays touched on our origins from the Chosen People. They had the Law, the Prophets, and the promise of the Christ, but we have the Christ as well. Today's readings recount for us the next step, the founding of the Church and the origin of the papacy.

The readings invite us to reflect, first on the Church and the role of the Pope; second, on God as Law-giver; and third, on the role of the ambassadors of Christ.

First, the Church and the role of Peter originated from God. Peter at last recognizes in Jesus the long-awaited Messiah. Jesus assures him that he did so only with the help of the Father. And at once, Jesus promises to found his Church, and to give it into the charge of Peter. ''You are Rock, and on this rock I will build my Church.'' In the Greek, the word *Rock* and the word *Peter* are one and the same. Simon's new name is Peter, that is, Rock.

We have here a twofold revelation which underlies our Catholic faith. The God-man will build a Church, and he will build it on Peter. The Church and the papacy originated from God.

Secondly, God is the original Lawgiver, and the source of all just law in both the Church and all human society. The great English legal authority, William Blackstone, stated that ''The law of nature . . . dictated by God himself . . . is binding . . . in all countries and at all times; no human law is of any validity, if contrary to this . . .'' This law of nature, which we know instinctively in many cases, is illustrated by the commandment, ''Thou shalt not murder.'' Every civilization has accepted it.

Our founding fathers followed the tradition put so well by Blackstone. In the Declaration of Independence they wrote, ''We hold these truths to be self-evident, that all men are created equal, that they are endowed by their Creator with certain unalienable Rights, that among these are Life, Liberty, and the pursuit of happiness.''

In a materialistic age, the hue and cry goes up, ''You can't legislate morality!'' But one must respond, ''What else is there to legislate but morality?'' All good laws, even speed laws, reduce to morality. It is true that we must restrict legislation to those laws which most people know by instinct. The law of the right to life is an example. That is why the Roe vs. Wade decision legalizing the killing of unborn children was so horrible. It flew in the face of the law of nature which our founding fathers expressed in the Declaration of Independence.

The role of the Church and the Pope is to teach God's law, both the law of nature and the law of faith. The Church does not originate the moral law; it only codifies it. Christ appointed the Pope with his assisting bishops to be interpreters and guardians of natural and revealed law.

The word *apostle* means *one who is sent*. Peter and the other apostles were sent by God to do their work. St. Paul the Apostle said that God ''entrusted the message of reconciliation to us. This makes us ambassadors of Christ.'' *Ambassadors* is the key word. The Pope does not stand on his own, or make laws on his own. He is the ambassador of Christ. He is the interpreter of the revelation under the guidance of the Holy Spirit.

It is difficult to be an ambassador of the absolute today. A chairman of a college philosophy department stated, ''I never talk to my students about the 'moral' thing to do.'' He added, ''It makes me sound like I'm standing on a pedestal, dispensing truth.'' But, if convinced of the truth of the natural law, must he not teach it? And, if he has found no truth, why is he teaching?

The Pope, the bishops, and the priests believe that they are ambassadors of the message of God. They believe they have the truth not as something they originated, but as the revelation communicated by God to the Church. They have authority over no one except those who freely submit themselves. Catholics submit themselves because they find in their conscience the call to the Church as the true Church of Christ.

Fr. Frank, in the novel I mentioned, is a confused priest. He need not and must not judge consciences. Popes, bishops and priests are forbidden to judge anyone's conscience. They are only commanded to form in the teaching of Christ the conscience of everyone who is Catholic. Even in the confessional, the penitent accuses himself. The priest's responsibility is to decide whether the penitent is trying to live by the law of Christ and his Church. If so, he administers the forgiveness of Christ, and the blessing and encouragement of Holy Mother the Church. I would urge Fr. Frank to get this clear in his mind, then pray to have the strength to preach the truth as the Church receives it. If a president must swear to uphold the Constitution, must not every pope, bishop and priest uphold the law of Christ the God-man?

Thirdly, the role of Ambassadors of Christ is to help us know the mind and heart of Christ. It is not easy, as Paul indicates, but he says to the Philippians, "Have this mind in you which is also in Christ Jesus." Certainly, Christ's promise to Peter gives assurance he will help Peter to know his mind as far as Peter must to do his work. The Pope studies, prays for the Spirit's guidance, and consults the revelation and the tradition and the living Church. Only then does he make his pronouncements. We must struggle in turn to understand and give consent.

All is directed to our being one with Christ in mind and heart and body. We receive life from him, and must be subject to him in love and adoration. There is one Lord, one faith, one baptism. We the Church are to show this for the salvation of all people and the glory of God the Father.

"A" — Twenty-second Sunday of the Year

Jr 20:7-9
Rm 12:1-2
Mt 16: 21-27

SUMMONS TO SUFFERING

In *The Apostle,* a great novel of St. Paul by Sholem Asch, Paul tries to convert the famous pagan philosopher, Seneca. Seneca is much impressed by this God who loves his creation enough to become a man to bring us joy and freedom. But he has a problem. Why, he asks, should God become a man who suffers and is slain? Why not rather become one of the great ones of the earth?

Paul cries out his questions in response: Who are the great ones? How do you measure greatness? By God's measure or man's? Are they great who seize power and debase others? Or rather, those who lift up the human species by heroic deeds even to the shedding of their own blood, as Jesus did?

Those are essentially the questions the readings call us to ponder. Let's reflect along three lines: Jesus mandates the acceptance of suffering with him; suffering with Jesus is a privilege; but how shall we endure it with joy, like the saints?

First, Jesus mandates suffering. The word is out: Unless we take up our cross, we can't walk with him. Do we view the mandate of the cross as a burden or a privilege? St. Peter thought it a privilege. It is said of Peter that when the Romans crucified him, he begged to be hung upside-down. He did not consider himself worthy to hang on the cross in the likeness of Christ.

Peter had come a long way, had he not? On first hearing Jesus' doctrine of suffering, all he could think of was to talk Jesus out of it. And, I might add, without any success. Only Jesus' resurrection brought him around.

Has faith brought us around, or is our attitude like Peter's earlier one? We often act as though the necessity or value of suffering is beyond understanding. Actually, a little reflection makes us see that to suffer with Christ is both a necessity and a privilege. Today and always, we need, like Peter, to ponder the purpose and meaning of suffering. No human being can escape it. Christ simply calls us to bear necessary suffering willingly.

Secondly, to suffer with Christ is an ennobling and rewarding privilege; it is also a necessity. Is it not a privilege to share in the companionship, the labors and the victories of the God-man? What greater privilege is there? What is more ennobling than to carry on our shoulders a share in Christ's labors? What is more honorable than to develop a noble soul that leaves nothing undone, whatever the cost? What is more uplifting than to lead others to resurrection and the fullness of life in God? What better preserves our own dignity than to lend Christ a hand in the work of our salvation and that of all people? Doesn't the whole world admire Mother Teresa of Calcutta's life of sacrifice for the poor and the dying?

The cross is a necessity with a purpose. To see that more clearly, let's look at some of the necessary sufferings. We will begin with the necessity of avoiding sin. We sin either to avoid suffering or to seize illicit pleasure. Clearly, to follow Christ, we must suffer rather than sin.

Next comes fidelity to Catholic doctrine. The teaching of Christ calls us to reject the world's sleazy way of life, and live by God's way. There is sacrifice involved in avoiding the world's lies and cheatings and immoral short cuts to pleasure. This is suffering with a meaning, even if the world mocks us.

Then there is the cross of being faithful to the duties of marriage and parenting, or those of priesthood and religious life.

Some abandon marriage when the first big troubles come. The true Christian dares every trial, and works through every hardship, knowing God himself wills that what he has joined together no man should put asunder. Love must always triumph.

Priests and religious also struggle to be faithful to their vocation. They, too, sometimes fail, but many more endure the trial. Jeremiah went through torment to be faithful. He spoke the prophetic word of God, but people did not want to hear its demands. He was mocked and punished and thrown down a well. So he resolved he would prophesy no more; but God's word burned in him like a fire and he went back and spoke it.

Whatever our chosen calling and state of life, all of us have the cross of sickness or disappointment or failure. All of us have the cross of our own sins and their consequences. We can turn bitter and resentful and hateful, or we can bear our cross with love, knowing that God can make it all work out for our good. All is in God's hands, and if we put ourselves in the hands of divine providence no suffering will be wasted.

Finally, how shall we bear suffering with joy, like the saints? We begin by pondering the necessity and purpose of suffering in a sinful world, as we've just done. We see that we and our destiny are greater than our suffering. It is beneath our dignity to manipulate ourselves to avoid necessary suffering.

We become aware that suffering is the work of sin, not of God. If the martyr who is faithful to God even to death is the glory of God, that is by way of exception, and his death is caused by sinners, not by God. In the ordinary course of events, the glory of God is men and women, girls and boys holy, healthy, happy and fully alive. We bring on much of our own suffering by spending too much, taking too little care of our health, and yielding to sin. Who does not see the suffering in the world brought on by these things? One woman said to St. Jane Frances De Chantal that she endured suffering "as an exercise which God sends." The saint responded, "We give ourselves, ordinarily, the troubles which we have."

We find joy in necessary suffering by keeping our eyes on Jesus and his example. "For the sake of the joy which lay before him he endured the cross, heedless of its shame. He has taken his seat at the right of the throne of God."

And we set before us Mary as the model of accepting the cross. If she did any running, it was not from the cross, but to the cross where Jesus hung. She certainly brought no witless sufferings on herself, but she was always ready to say, "Be it done to me according to your will." In that there is joy, even in suffering.

"A" — Twenty-third Sunday of the Year   Ezk 33:7-9
                                                          Rm 13:8-10
                                                          Mt 18:15-20

GIVING AND RECEIVING CORRECTION

Jesus has left us a problem. On the one hand he said, "Judge not." On the other, he tells us to correct another when he wrongs us. Now, how can we correct if we can't judge? The answer is that we cannot and must not judge consciences, but we can and must judge deeds. We can't know whether a person *realizes* he is doing wrong, but we can often *see* when he does wrong.

To give correction is hard for most of us. We feel in need of correction ourselves. Even Pope St. Gregory the Great felt that way. He said that in giving correction he denounced himself, and added, "I cannot preach with any competence, and yet insofar as I succeed, still I myself do not live my life according to my own preaching."

One priest said, "Sometimes I feel like a hypocrite. I preach perfection, and sometimes I don't live it myself." His fellow priest said, "Preach it. It is your responsibility." There's an important principle here. To fail in the one responsibility is no excuse for failing in the other.

To give brotherly correction is a duty, and to receive it is a duty. Which is the harder? An honest answer tells us a lot about our own personality.

Today's readings invite us to reflect on three propositions. First, Jesus gave brotherly correction, and his priests must give it.

Secondly, at times all must give it. Thirdly, it must be done wisely and lovingly.

First, Jesus gave correction, and his priests must give it. In last Sunday's Gospel Jesus sternly corrected Peter when he denied that Jesus was going to suffer. Jesus said, "Get out of my sight, you satan!" Jesus freed the woman taken in adultery, but said, "From now on do not sin any more." He censured his apostles for failure to use good sense. He corrected St. Paul for persecuting him in his body, the Church. So Jesus not only preached correction; he practiced it.

Jesus' priests must do likewise. In the first reading, God warns the prophet Ezekiel that if he doesn't do his job of correcting sinners, he will be held responsible along with them. Priests have inherited this role. It would be better not to be a priest than to fail to do the work of a priest.

The priest's duty of giving correction is not easy, but it is necessary. To withhold it is to share the guilt of those who need it. Whether people like it or not, whether the priest likes it or not, it has to be done. What good is a watchdog that does not bark? Better to have none than be lulled into a false sense of security that could cost you your life. How much worse, then, is a priest without a bark who could cost people their eternity!

Secondly, there are roles and times in which everyone has to give brotherly correction. Parents have the duty of giving it to their children. And, what is so terribly hard, children sometimes have to give it to their parents. Teachers have to give it to their students; friends have to give it to friends.

Citizens have to give it to the nation. Who were the good people who did not speak out during the Holocaust in Germany? How many are failing to speak out during our own abortion holocaust? This is one case in which we all have a solemn duty of giving correction to our fellow citizens and our government. Vatican II called abortion and infanticide "unspeakable crimes." We don't have to judge the consciences of our fellow citizens, but we have to correct their consciences in the name of God and of humanity.

Thirdly, brotherly correction must be done wisely and lovingly. Much as most of us dread and fear giving correction, some people enjoy it and make a habit of it. They need correction themselves. Some give it only when they're so angry they can't hold back. They give it not so much to correct as to get relief.

St. Augustine warns us against false correction. He says, "Men are hopeless creatures, and the less they concentrate on their own sins, the more interested they become in the sins of others. They seek to criticize, not to correct. Unable to excuse themselves, they are ready to accuse others."

How then should we correct a brother? Jesus explains it. You get him alone, and point out the fault. Notice it is not done in a fit of anger, or in public, or out of hatred. If he rejects correction, you face him with two or three others. If even that doesn't work, refer it to the Church.

If married couples followed these directions, more marriages would survive. A couple with a serious falling out who can't settle it between them should sit down with their pastor. When we hear complaints against us with a third set of ears listening, it's amazing how it can begin to sound much more convincing, even before the third person gives us his considered opinion.

Jesus ends this matter of correction with a promise that the prayer of two or three joined together will be answered. Is he not telling us to pray with the offender for light for both?

When should we not correct? When we know that the offender reacts to correction the way dynamite reacts to a match. That ought to make us realize the person likely needs, not correction, but help. Isn't that often the case where there is alcohol or drug addiction? The only answer may lie in prayer and love and planning and consultation with experts.

I sum up with A Dozen Guidelines for Brotherly Correction:

1) Unless you are a model correction taker, be slow to give it.

2) Correct like a friend and fellow sinner, not like an enemy.
3) Knowing how you resent unjust correction, never inflict it.
4) Harping on past faults is not correction but condemnation.
5) Know that love wins over better than an army of accusations.
6) Get help to correct when it is needed.
7) Frame the correction so it will heal and not wound further.
8) Decide first whether the person needs correction or help.
9) Correct infrequently, and only the greater failings.
10) Correction hurts, so don't correct with a sledgehammer.
11) Think how prayerfully Mary would correct, and imitate her.
12) Put yourself in the culprit's shoes and think about it. You may
end up congratulating him for not being worse!

"A" — Twenty-fourth Sunday of the Year   Si 27:30-28:7
                                                        Rm 14:7-9
                                                        Mt 18:21-35

THE MATURE CHRISTIAN'S
FORGIVING HEART

We begin with a question. What is it which alone can remove
every sin, heal every breach and end every estrangement? What but
forgiveness? Forgiveness alone can do it. And we have it in
abundance from our kind God and Savior. By his tender forgiveness he has made this earth the land of beginning again. He has
done it not just by his forgiveness but by ours. He calls us all to be
forgivers like him. He has even put a kind of wonderful brag on our
lips, making us say to our Heavenly Father, "Father, forgive us our
trespasses as we forgive those who trespass against us."

What if we did that perfectly? What would we be like? Ulcers
would become an extinct species. Headaches would so decline that
Bayer Aspirin might go out of business. Husbands and wives

would become lovers again. Divorce lawyers would have to change their profession. Parents and children would become the best of friends. Our houses would radiate joy and ring with laughter.

And what would happen to our earth? If we ceased exporting unforgiveness from our homes into the world, hatred would begin to dim. The lights would go on again all over the world. The whole world would become a land of beginning again. How beautiful it would be for our world if Christ's forgiveness prevailed in our homes.

With that as our goal, let us reflect on the motives for forgiveness, the obstacles to forgiveness, and the rewards of forgiveness.

We begin with the motives. It is our Lord's own command. He hopes, wishes and wills that we be like him in forgiveness. If we love him, that is motive enough, but let's go on. It is the necessary thing to do. Unless we forgive, we won't be forgiven. Further, it is the godly thing to do. One little catechism asks, "Can we be like God?" The answer is that we can be like God, for St. John says that when we see him, we shall become like to him. This is the mystery of the grace of baptism. By forgiving, we *act* like the children of the heavenly Father which we have become. Finally, it is the way home. Every time we forgive, we move at least one step closer to our Father's eternal home.

Now we look at the obstacles to being more forgiving. The first obstacle is a desire for vengeance. We don't think people should "get away with it," as we say. We want to pay them back, we want justice. But the Lord says to us in the Scriptures, "Vengeance is mine." That is the only sensible thing, if we can judge only deeds and not guilt, as I reminded you last week in talking about brotherly correction. So let us put vengeance out of our hearts and forgiveness in its place.

The next obstacle is materialism and greed. When someone offends us, he takes something from us. It may be a snippet of our reputation, a book that belongs to us, a dent in our fender, or the quiet of our day. Whatever it is, if we are too attached to the things of this earth, forgiveness is not in our hearts. Only when we store up treasures in heaven do we escape slavery to the things of earth. Then forgiveness becomes easy, because what the offender robs from us is no great loss.

Another obstacle to forgiveness is lack of an understanding heart. You know that when you and I offend someone else, we can offer a whole litany of excuses that may all be true: "I had a headache, I was just feeling out of sorts, the boss was mean to me today, my rent is due," etc. An understanding heart realizes other people have those weaknesses too, and that if we are ready and willing to forgive ourselves, we should be ready and willing to forgive others. An understanding heart comes with the Holy Spirit's gifts of knowledge and piety. We should pray for those gifts. They help us understand the weakness of others by remembering our own before we became mature Christians. Then, like grown-up brothers and sisters of Jesus, we will be understanding toward those who haven't grown up.

The next obstacle is the failure to remember that death is on our doorstep. It may enter today, or decades down the line. When it enters, we will appear before God. Wouldn't it be wonderful if in that hour we can say to him, "Father, I've forgiven everyone as I hope you will forgive me." Wouldn't that be a cause for joy though? Picture the Father thinking, "He's only flesh and blood, and he always forgave! I don't have a leg to stand on. He reminds me of my Son!"

We can't omit as an obstacle the failure to meditate enough on Jesus crucified. There he is, crucified for our sins, crucified by us, holding out his arms even in death to forgive us and receive us back. There, we can all learn forgiveness.

Now we look at a few of the rewards of forgiveness. The first is that we too will be forgiven. I can take it for granted we all know we need it. Another reward is peace, peace of heart. It is not what others do to us that destroys our peace; it is how we respond. As we become peacemakers, our peace grows. We can't all become St. Francis of Assisi but we can all try. We'll at least make it part way. That is better than no way at all.

Jesus himself promised the next reward, when he said, "Blessed are the peacemakers, they will be called the children of God." Isn't it wonderful thinking of God being proud of you or me? It can happen.

A more immediate reward is to be able to say to Our Lord in Holy Communion, "I've been trying to do all that forgiving you want of me. It's sure a struggle, but it's great."

Let's close with the reward of family joy. Forgiving families become like the Holy Family. They are imitators of Jesus, Mary and Joseph. Within the walls of such a home, there are no grudges, no resentful glances, no throwing up of old faults, no sullen silences, no tension headaches, no interminable fatigue. There is instead a growing knowledge of the family of the Father, Son and Holy Spirit, even when they are not aware of it; for they are growing like the Holy Trinity, in whose image the family is made. So try forgiveness for a day. Then try it every day. Practice makes perfect.

"A" — Twenty-fifth Sunday of the Year

Is 55:6-9
Ph 1:20-24, 27
Mt 20:1-16

ATTITUDES OF THE MATURE CHRISTIAN

The problem of unemployment never goes away. How long ago Jesus told today's parable of unemployment! And today people walk our streets and the streets of the world looking for work. Though socialism was supposed to eliminate it, the Chinese and Russians are wrestling with unemployment.

But this parable is not primarily about unemployment at all; it is about attitudes proper to a mature Christian. In the past two weeks, we've reflected on how mature Christians administer brotherly correction, and how they offer forgiveness.

Now we ask: What is a mature Christian's attitude toward the distribution of God's gifts, and the use of his own? We will look for answers by considering the primary meaning of Jesus' parable, then go on to the lessons of charity it teaches us, and the way to apply them.

The primary purpose of the parable about the vineyard is to instruct us in the way God distributes his gifts. The owner outrages his employees by giving the late-hired workers as much as the first-hired. Notice, I did not say "by paying them as much," but "by giving them as much."

Many people still think this is unfair. In a home Mass, a priest pointed out that the owner did nothing illegal. If the employees sued him, they would be laughed out of court. But the priest's mother cried out, "The union would get after him!"

The Gospel can offend our legalistic sense of justice. A lawyer later told that same priest that he used to feel uneasy about the parable until he suddenly saw its deeper justice.

Scripture scholars tell us that the first meaning of the parable has nothing to do with money. Jesus told the parable to the Jewish people. They were the ones who had struggled through the ages bearing the burden of serving God, the vineyard owner. Now Jesus was telling them that at the Final Judgment the wages of salvation were to be given to these late-comers as well.

Is that outrageous? Or were they forgetting that neither the Covenant nor faith nor first grace is earned? The best things in life are free. The Jews retain the honor of being the Chosen People, the first called; but they are not the only ones called. In any case, God gives his gifts as he pleases.

Now let us change the parable. You are the employer, and a good person. All day you've been hiring people. An hour before quitting time, you find your brother walking the streets looking for work, and hire him. When the wages are handed out, you slip him a full day's pay. What could be more natural, more kind, more just? Well, let us remember that the men who came last in the parable were Christ's brothers, for every man is his brother.

What lesson of charity does this parable teach us? Surely it should teach us that God's ways are not so far above our ways that we can't imitate them. Jesus said we must become perfect like our heavenly Father. Every man is *our* brother too. Even atheistic governments give support to those in need.

Perhaps you really are an employer, a master of one of God's vineyards. Then remember that, as a brother or sister of Christ, you have every man for your brother too. Treat them accordingly.

We know that Jesus the Carpenter of Nazareth would find at least a few hours' work for an unemployed man; and Joseph and Mary would never refuse food to the hungry.

The endangered unborn, the poor, the sick, and the homeless are brothers and sisters of us all. When we cast our vote for the government leaders who say yes or no to their needs, let us remember that.

One day each of us will leave his or her body and be homeless indeed. Unless the Father of All raises our bodies, our very souls will have no home. Unless he opens his eternal home to us, we will go to a place which no man would willingly call home. Then let us do for others what we hope he will do for us.

How can we apply this lesson more broadly? We need the clear vision to see that the works of justice will be overwhelmed by the needs unless we correct the root causes of poverty and disorder in our society. We must do the works of justice, but they will be swamped if our faith is defective, as it is in many.

Contrary to God's law, the defective faith of some accepts both premarital sex and divorce-remarriage. These are the very sins that produce many of the single-parent families which are impoverishing the country faster than the works of justice can move. Irresponsible sex is both a sin and a social disaster.

Heroic single parents struggling to raise children should be praised, and fathers compelled to help. But the circumstances which threw so many into this struggle need to be warded off or millions more will share their lot. A billboard in one city has this message for the young: "Don't be a loser. No sex till marriage." That was God's advice and command all along. Don't be a loser by losing God.

Socially active Christians who make it sound as though the only sin is not to be socially active are not the solution. They are part of the problem. They are applying bandaids without removing the infection which is causing the disease.

People who give money for charity do well, but the mature Christian does more. Popes and bishops have urged us to make our values felt throughout society. This means choosing careers and positions that have social consequences. In our highly organized society, we have to think of serving Christ in larger terms.

Shouldn't we hear Christ saying: "I was ignorant and you became a teacher. I was hungry and you became a farmer. I was downtrodden and you became a politician who cared. I was homeless and you became a builder concerned to build houses the poor could afford. I was a street kid and you opened a hospice. I contracted AIDS and you worked to research a cure. I feared nuclear annihilation, and you worked for peace. I didn't know right from wrong, and you became a religious sister to educate me. I was hungry for God and you became a priest. I lacked both body and soul and you became my parents." If we think in these terms we will offer God and the world something really worthwhile.

"A" — Twenty-sixth Sunday of the Year   Ezk 18:25-28
Ph 2:1-11
Mt 21:28-32

HOW TO BE A GOOD CATHOLIC?

What's more important in a fruit tree, that it have a good appearance, or that it bear good fruit? Wouldn't we expect any farmer to say that good fruit is more important? Now a second question: What's more important, that fruit look good, or that it be good for you? Surely, that it be good for you. Yet in 1989 the Environmental Protection Agency found that a chemical used to preserve the *appearance* of apples might cause cancer. The chemical gets into the flesh of the apple and can't be washed off. Yet it was being used on about five percent of the nation's red apples. We fruit eaters surely would say that it's more important that fruit be good than that it look good.

That is essentially what Jesus is saying about believers. At the Last Supper he said, "I am the vine, you the branches. Whoever remains in me and I in him will bear much fruit." The good fruit of human beings which Jesus is talking about is of course faith, hope, and the good works of love. Today's readings condemn those who have merely the good appearance of religion and praise those who have the good fruit of religion. That raises for us the question, What does it take to be a good Catholic?

Let's probe further by considering, first, that love of God is found more in deeds than in words or appearances; second, that Jesus praised those who had the fruit of religion, not its show; and third, that to be good is to be like Jesus.

We begin, then, with the fact that love of God is found more in deeds than in words or appearances, or even past performance. The people described in the first reading had done what pleased God. Now they have decided they've stored up enough merits to please themselves and still be acceptable. God informs them that a good life is never a license to lead a bad one. A genuinely good life leads to a better one. Life with God is not a bank account; it is a love affair, and a family relationship. Perhaps we, like God, have had friends who suddenly proved to be friends no longer, or even became enemies. Similarly, the virtuous person who has lost his love is no longer a friend of God. He has died spiritually. God will keep calling, but unless he repents, there can be no friendship.

On the other hand, the sinner who repents becomes the friend of God. Jesus made many such friends among tax collectors and prostitutes. The religious leaders were horrified at this, but Jesus tells them that these repentant sinners are more pleasing to God than they.

The story of the two sons exposes the roots of the disorder. The elder puts on the show of being a good son. Sure, dad, whatever you want, right away! And that's as far as it goes. No doubt he always has a hundred excuses, but the fact remains that there is no good fruit. The other son doesn't have the beauty of the shining red apple with the poison finish. In a rebellious moment, he refuses to obey. But he has a good heart and feels bad, and goes and does what he was told.

A mannequin with a beautiful set of clothes is still no fashion model. It is dead. A show of religion without faith and love is just as dead. The religious leaders had too much show, and not enough substance. The tax collectors and prostitutes lacked the show but had the substance. When the Baptizer warned of God's displeasure, they heard and did God's will.

Jesus praised those who had the fruit of religion, not its show. He honored those who believed in God's righteousness, not their own. He loved those who had the substance of religion, not its pretense. Let's consider further that son who had mere show. One priest asked a number of children, ''What do you think is the worst sin?'' It is surprising how many said, ''Lying.'' The pretense of religion has something in common with lying. One is not what one seems. The skin of the apple is beautiful, but what do you taste when you bite into it?

There are subtle ways to take on the show of religion and avoid its burdens. Many today claim to love our Faith, but disagree with certain teachings of the Church. Their dissent can and may put them in the position of having the show of the Faith, but not its substance. How can we both believe and not believe?

When the Pope was here in 1987, Cardinal Bernardin told him that "many American Catholics, given the freedom that they have enjoyed for more than two centuries, almost instinctively react negatively when they are told that they must do something, even though in their hearts they may know that they should do it."

The Holy Father, in one of his talks, said, "It is sometimes reported that a large number of Catholics today do not adhere to the teaching of the Church on a number of questions, notably sexual and conjugal morality, divorce and remarriage. Some are reported as not accepting the Church's clear teaching on abortion. It has also been noted that there is a tendency on the part of some Catholics to be selective in their adherence to the Church's moral teachings. It is sometimes claimed that dissent from the magisterium is totally compatible with being a 'good Catholic' and poses no obstacle to the reception of the sacraments. This is a grave error that challenges the teaching office of the bishops of the United States and elsewhere."

Where would Jesus put each of us U.S. Catholics? With the Pharisees who had too little substance and too much show? Or with the believers who had the substance if not the show?

To be good is to be like Jesus. That's the long and short of it. What would Jesus do if he were in my shoes? Then I'll do it. He wants substance, not show. Though God, he joined our humble human state. Though king, he served us. Though Author of life, he died for us. He came to make us one with him, one flock and one Shepherd. What does that say of private interpretation of the Faith? Faith in the beginning made believers one mind and one heart.

Jesus asks us what we ask of anyone close to us, that love be not show but substance. I think none of us intends to give him less. But unless we avoid the pitfalls of the people in today's readings, we will give him less. So let us remember that to be a good Catholic is to be like Jesus and Mary.

"A" — Twenty-seventh Sunday of the Year   Is 5:1-7
Ph 4:6-9
Mt 21:33-43

PROUD GUARDIANS OF LIFE

To stars and stones the Creator gave existence. To plants he gave life, and to animals, feeling. To us he gave existence, life, feeling, intelligence, freedom, and eternal life.

"To be or not to be: that is the question," says Shakespeare's Hamlet. Is it better to live, or to commit suicide and escape life's troubles? That was Hamlet's question. He chose life only from fear of what might await him after death.

In today's readings, Isaiah decries bloodshed, and Jesus tells the parable which prophesies his own murder. The readings invite us to appreciate the sacred gift of life, and denounce all unjust taking of life. And so three questions: Does human society respect the inviolability of life? Is life ours absolutely or in stewardship? Is a life of suffering worth living or not?

First, then, does human society respect the inviolable and inestimable gift of life? The fact is that the U.S. flings back into God's face the lives of well over a million of its unborn children each year. Our society has lost its respect for life.

Why? A pro-choice, that is pro-abortion, medical journal, *California Medicine,* explains why. The journal states that the Judeo-Christian ethic which held each life sacred is collapsing.

People are concerned about the population problem, and the limits of resources, and in addition want a higher quality life. So they have opted for abortion, thus revising traditional Western morality. The journal says that since we haven't yet quite disposed of the old ethic, people pretend that abortion isn't really killing. Then it adds, and I quote, "The result has been a curious avoidance of the scientific fact, which everyone really knows, that human life begins at conception and is continuous whether intra- or extra-uterine until death." What honest person can still pretend abortion isn't the taking of human life, when a pro-abortion journal brazenly says it is?

Babies are now looked over in the womb. Some that don't measure up are killed. Even anti-abortion people are using contraceptive pills which the manufacturers tell us sometimes work by abortion. Modern Natural Family Planning has been shown to be as effective, but who is listening? Courses in Natural Family Planning are given in most dioceses, but few learn it.

The killing doesn't stop with the unborn. Babies born disabled, and aborted babies born alive, are sometimes left unfed and uncared for until they die. In specific cases, courts have approved withholding even food and water from the seriously ill. The Hemlock Society is pressing for the legalizing of suicide. In the Netherlands doctors are annually killing five to ten thousand AIDS-infected and other ill people at their own request.

Clearly, human life is no longer treated as sacred. Our growing children sense this, and act on it. Suicides among the young have skyrocketed. So have drugs, drink, and reckless driving, which are slower ways of reaching the same end.

Secondly, is life ours absolutely or only in stewardship? It is ours only in stewardship, for God says, "Thou shalt not kill." Does this prohibition include the self, the unborn, the old, the disabled? Clearly, it does. God makes no exception, nor does the Church. And one day we and our society will be judged by the divine Lawgiver.

When Pope John Paul II visited this country in 1987, he extolled it from its majestic mountains to its quest for excellence. Then he added, "If you want equal justice for all, and true freedom and lasting peace, then, America, defend life!"

The Pope saw our good efforts for refugees, minorities, and disarmament. He said, "All this will succeed only if respect for life and its protection by law is granted to every human being from conception until natural death." He declared that the abortion issue is the most important test of the U.S. as a free nation. We can see why. We claim to protect life, liberty, and the pursuit of happiness. But is it not done selectively, so that powerless persons like unborn babies need not apply?

Thirdly and most crucially, is a life of suffering worth living or not? We say it is. We claim to believe that Christ's suffering redeemed the world. We profess with St. Paul that we must carry on his saving suffering, for we are his body. We claim to believe, then, that suffering has serious and immense meaning. It is part of life's pilgrimage from conception through natural death to eternal life. Prayers, works, joys and sufferings are all part of a divine plan that leads to God. Suffering puts us in special relationship with the Heart of our suffering Redeemer.

Cannot we who see the nobility and dignity of suffering for the sake of love and life not help others? Cannot we lift out of their despair those who measure life's value only by its freedom from pain? One writer proposed that if a child would have less suffering from abortion than from living as an unwanted child, it would be more merciful to kill him. Can't he see that all of us would have less pain if we were killed? But what of the lost joy, pleasure, opportunity, hope, beauty, and truth? What of the lost chance to love, serve, and contribute to the work of Christ and the good of society, and to merit everlasting life?

When Pope Paul VI died, his will described the beauty of creation: "I am closing my eyes on this sorrowful, dramatic and magnificent world, calling down on it, once again, divine Goodness.'' In touching words, he sang the praise of life: ''In the face of death, the total and definitive separation from the present life, I feel the need to celebrate the gift, the fortune, the beauty, the destiny of this fleeting existence! Lord, I thank you who have called me to life.''

Jesus foretells the taking of his life; Isaiah denounces bloodshed; Mary and Joseph flee Bethlehem to safeguard the life of the Son of God. Let us too flee the evils that threaten life, and defend all who are threatened by an unjust death. Bear with suffering as the blessed cross of Christ. Reaffirm the articles of faith, appreciate the joy of life, seize the hope of eternal glory in the life of God forever. As faithful stewards of life, we will overflow with it in the chambers of our Father's house.

''A'' — Twenty-eighth Sunday of the Year

Is 25:6-10
Ph 4:12-14, 19-20
Mt 22:1-14

ANTICIPATING HEAVEN'S JOY

A priest raised the topic of heaven and hell, but his non-believing friend promptly denied life after death. ''You have a losing position,'' the priest said. ''If you're right, we'll never know. If I'm right, I can say, 'I told you so.' ''

A certain French writer refused to discuss the topic. ''I have friends in both places,'' he explained. A BBC producer wrote a priest-consultant asking how to get official Roman Catholic views on heaven and hell. The answer came in one word: ''Die.'' That would certainly work, but I propose an easier way: Listen.

What will it be like to enter heaven? A priest who visited the Holy Land had an experience that helps. In a Jerusalem Chapel he saw on a banner the words of Psalm 123, ''And now my feet are standing within your gates, O Jerusalem." Only at that moment was he struck in all force with the fact: He was actually walking where the Lord walked. He had a sense of unreality. He wanted to say, "Pinch me. It can't be true!" That sense of an experience too great to be real persisted for months. It seemed like a dress rehearsal for heaven, as Psalm 126 puts it: "When the Lord brought back the captives of Zion, we were like men dreaming."

In that first reading, Isaiah says something similar. People in heaven will say, "Behold our God, to whom we looked to save us . . . Let us rejoice and be glad that he has saved us." Note that wonderful change of tense. It is no longer, "He will save us," but "He has saved us." Surely, that will be the first and overwhelming realization, and rather than months, it may last forever. We risen, death dead, and joy undying.

In keeping with the three readings, let's ask three questions about heaven: How do we get there? What will it be like? Whom do we want to take with us?

How do we get there? The Gospel parable says how, but before considering it, consider this: philosophers say that "everything that acts, acts to obtain something." The purpose of the act of religion is to find life with God. In the parable, Jesus tells us that we find that life with God by accepting the invitation of his messengers, and putting on the wedding garment.

Whom did you identify with in the parable? The people who responded, or the ones too busy to respond? The people who wore the wedding garment, or the one who didn't? Did you sympathize with the loving king and his son, or with his enemies?

Clearly, the messengers are his prophets, his Son, and his Son's apostles, who founded the Church. By accepting and living the invitation, we will arrive one day at our Father's House. The wedding garment is sanctifying grace, with which baptism cloaks our souls. It can be torn off only by mortal sin.

What will heaven be like? Isaiah describes it as a luscious banquet. Jesus gives us an update. It is the wedding banquet of

God's own Son. St. Paul adds another fact. The bride is his people, the Church. The first gift of Bridegroom to bride is eternal life. ''I am the resurrection and the life.''

That reminds us that we will be there in our risen bodies. What will they be like? No eye has seen, no ear heard, no mind or heart conceived the marvel of them, as St. Paul tells us. If that be true of bodies, how much more are the spiritual realities beyond our grasp! But this we can say: Heaven will exceed every desire for love or joy or pleasure that anyone has.

Are some troubled because Jesus said that in heaven marriage will be obsolete? That's because God has prepared a union of love excelling earthly marriage as heaven excels earth. On earth, man and woman were made in the likeness of God. In heaven, they will be as God. Jesus promised he will say, ''Enter into the joy of your Lord.'' That joy is God's own. ''From your delightful stream,'' says Psalm 36, ''you give them to drink. For with you is the fountain of life, and in your light we see light.''

The light here is the light divine. ''This is eternal life,'' Jesus said, ''to know you, the one true God, and Jesus Christ whom you have sent.'' To see this Light is to flame with its glory, as diamonds flame in the sun. We are God's small children now, John says, but haven't been told what we shall be. ''We do know,'' he adds, ''that when it is revealed we shall be like him, for we shall see him as he is.''

We shall see the God of loveliness, and find out what it really means to adore, in a meltdown of love no earthling has ever known. We will see and embrace the mystery of the three divine Persons, and their oneness as God. We ourselves will be united to God, as only divine love can unite.

We'll see and embrace our Virgin Mother Mary. We will hobnob with all our favorite saints and angels. We will have the freedom to do at last whatever we please. Being like God, we will have the power to do it, and being good like God, desire nothing evil.

Thirdly, whom do we want to take with us? Before answering that question, let me ask another. In today's parable, did you identify only with those who were called, or also with those who did the calling? By God's plan, we are all callers as well as called. When Jesus said, "Go, therefore, and make disciples of all nations," he included all of us in the work.

Whom do we want to take with us? Everybody! Paul says God our Savior "wills everyone to be saved and to come to the knowledge of the truth." Preaching alone won't do it. Living with concern to promote love and justice and kindness is necessary. That's why the Church wants us involved in social affairs. Jesus is the new Adam, and we the new creation, already here on earth. That is why Vatican II said that as children of God we should be more concerned about earthly affairs than worldlings.

It should be clear, then, that there are no disappointments in heaven. If the Bread of Heaven we eat here on earth at Mass is already beyond anything we could have hoped, what will the Bread be like in heaven itself — not to mention the other courses! And don't think you won't feel at home there. Anyone who has truly tasted the love of Jesus Christ in the Eucharist will certainly be no stranger in Paradise.

"A" — Twenty-ninth Sunday of the Year

Is 45:1, 4-6
1 Th 1:1-5
Mt 22:15-21

ONE BILLION MISSIONARIES

You may remember how people became involved when little Jessica McClure fell down a narrow well beyond quick rescue. Those far and near prayed; those close by brought assistance and worked for days until at last the brave little girl was up and in their arms. In a manifest emergency the world shows its love and kindness.

By faith we know there is an emergency more awful but less manifest. Adam's sin plunged the whole world into a well of sin and death. There is no escape except through Christ's grace.

Did little Jessica know any more than that she was stuck in darkness without love or help until at last her rescue came? People in the well of sin and death often know even less of their plight. Many know nothing of the hope of life eternal.

When a doctor finds a cure for some dread disease, he cannot rest until the remedy reaches the ill. But he needs the help of others or it never will. God sent his Son as the universal remedy for all peoples; but he wants his Son to depend on us, his brothers and sisters, to carry it to the world. By God's plan, there are over a billion Christian missionaries, for every one of us is called to spread the Good News of the cure Christ brings.

"Give to God what is God's," Jesus says in today's Gospel. We owe to God this service of making Christ's salvation known. Do we not feel we could not live without the love, light, forgiveness and hope that Christ and his Church bring? Then how can we neglect all those others down in that dark well?

"How can I be a missionary?" seems to be the reaction of many Christians. They think the only sane response is a hurried admission that they can't. But do they realize that at first even Moses, Isaiah and Peter fell into their same error?

When God chose to send Moses as his spokesman, Moses objected, "Who am I that I should go?" And he added, "I've never been eloquent." But God replied that he is the one who made the tongue, and Moses went. When Isaiah had the vision that called him, he cried, "Woe is me, I'm doomed . . . a man of unclean lips." Then God's angel purified his lips with a burning coal, and Isaiah preached. Peter knelt before Jesus and said, "Depart from me, Lord, for I am a sinful man." Jesus said in reply, " I will make you fishers of men." And Peter fished.

God sent these three despite their feelings, and they proved to be three of his great missionaries. The lesson? It is that what God wants of us he does in us if we respond, for he is God.

In today's first reading, God reveals that he sent King Cyrus to do his will without so much as telling Cyrus. Are we not more blessed if we know and give our *yes?*

The answer to the question, "How can I be a missionary?" is, Keep the faith, live the faith, and give the faith.

First, keep the faith and grow in it. Peter drew people to Jesus because he had strong faith in Jesus. Paul spread the faith because he spoke "in complete conviction." Keep the faith, then, by listening to the Church and believing the Church's God-given word, as did Peter and Paul. If we have faith, it radiates, and spreads. Some years ago a national magazine described in a kind of amazement how Catholics flock to Mass and the Eucharist because they believe that Jesus is truly present in the Eucharist. The faith radiates and catches fire in other hearts if it is aflame in our own. But we must deepen faith by prayer and sacrament. It is our way of living with Jesus as Peter did.

Second, live the faith. Fulfill the duty of Mass on Sunday without fail. Go to Mass daily if you have the love and opportunity. Uphold marriage and family values by word and example. Use your vote to reject abortion, pornography, euthanasia, drugs, and all the other spreading evils. Use the vote to help the homeless, the unemployed, the needy. One woman interviewed at election time said, "I leave religion out of the voting booth." Now how can we leave God out of anything? Or shall we leave him out at the very time we can serve him best? Should we not say, "Lord, enlighten me to go into this polling booth and vote as would you"?

One man who married a non-Catholic woman quietly carried on his Catholic life without display or fanfare. After some years, she freely chose to convert. Example is the most powerful form of missionary work.

Thirdly, give the faith. Having it and living it are not enough.

The faith spread to us or our ancestors through the tireless labors of uncounted apostles, preachers and martyrs. Those labors must go on in us. The faith we freely received, we must freely give.

Is there a sense of emptiness in your life? That is often the way a call to do God's work begins. Do you ever feel sick to death of building your own little kingdom, and wish to build a greater kingdom? You can and should. We are all called to build God's kingdom.

How? Become a priest, sister, brother, or lay apostle. Start in your own parish. Examine your financial contribution to the parish. Do you give what you can to its needs, its works of mercy, its help to foreign missions? Remember that when you give, you help the work of missionaries who give their very lives.

Someone might say, "I have neither health nor money." You can still give as much as anyone. Offer daily all your prayers, works, joys and sufferings to the Heart of Jesus in the Mass for all his purposes. The Little Flower, St. Therese of Lisieux, became a contemplative sister. She never went to the missions, but she prayed so ardently the Church made her the world patron of the missions.

The world has endless need to be helped in the name of Christ, but its greatest need is the need for Christ himself. Would we want to be without him? Then let's not fail those others who need our help to learn of him. Today we ask ourselves, "What have I done for Christ? What am I doing for Christ? What will I do for Christ?"

"A" — Thirtieth Sunday of the Year   Ex 2:20-26
1 Th 1:5-10
Mt 22:34-40

MADE FOR LOVE

One day there came parading through an airport terminal a lovely little girl with a great purple heart flaming on her blouse. Emblazoned across the purple heart were the words, "Made for love." To look at her was to believe it.

Since we're not all pretty little girls, it's not as easy to believe that we were all made for love. Yet God commands us to do only that for which he made us, and in today's Gospel Jesus commands us to love. He tells us that all God's revelation and laws come down to the command to love. It shouldn't surprise us, for God patterned us after himself, and he simply commands us to become what he made us, lovers in his image and likeness.

What surprises some is the idea that love can be commanded. How can love be commanded? What is love that it can be commanded? How can we grow in the love of God and neighbor that is commanded? Let's reflect on these questions.

How can love be commanded? The question arises because of the romantic notion that love just happens. One doesn't work to love, one just *falls* in love, so how can we be commanded to love? We meet that special person, and love comes welling up like water from an artesian well. It's all very mysterious and very beautiful. But if we sit around and wait for all our love to come from artesian wells, we'll have a drought of love. It's no more practical than the person who refuses to work to earn a living because he expects to win the lottery.

A little thought easily answers the question of how we can be commanded to love. Falling in love is the most pleasant way, but experience teaches us that there are many ways to come to love. Sometimes, at first meeting, we dislike a person for as trivial a reason as the way he wears his hat. But if we put aside such worthless feelings, and get to know the man, we begin to discover likeable things about him, and before long we develop the love of friendship. Again, someone we dislike comes to us with a need. Because we are not mean, we try to help. In the process, we discover in him good qualities we never noticed before, like humility and gratitude. Before long we like him, and even feel like an older brother or sister toward him.

What, then, is love that it can be commanded? St. Thomas Aquinas says the beginning of love is to wish another well. Since we're all children of God, we can see how that can be commanded. But if we wish another well, we must refrain from harming him, cheating him, or extorting from him, as the first reading states. That too is love. The Ten Commandments really say that you must love your neighbor at least enough not to harm him in any way.

But if one whom we wish well needs help only we can give, to wish him well without helping is too empty. God commands the love that aids his well-being. And we find that when we give that help, love for him grows of itself.

Love is mysterious, and we can't define or describe it completely, but let's go deeper. We can describe its action. To love is to go in search of the good and once we find it hold to it from the heart. When we learn more about that good truth or appealing person, we love it the more. If we come to the point of holding to it body and soul, we have found deep love.

What does this tell us but that love can be commanded because we can cultivate love like a garden? Courtship is a good example. When a boy and girl meet and date, it is often simply because they like one another. But as they go together, they begin to discover all those endearing young charms, and if they are blessed, they find one day that they have fallen in love.

What's coming out is that if we want to we can cultivate love for anyone, even an enemy. We can grow in love by practicing it, like any virtue. A virtue is a good action we practice until it becomes a habit. And love is the greatest of the virtues.

Love is worth the time it takes to grow, whether it be love of husband or wife, son or daughter, father or mother, brother or sister, or any of the children of God. Above all and in all, love of God is the love to cultivate.

How grow in love of God and neighbor? Let us begin with love of God. Cultivate knowledge of the qualities in God which attract us all naturally: love, beauty, truth, goodness, innocence, and the happiness and pleasure this knowledge brings. Meditate on the passion of Jesus, which is like looking at pure love in action. Think about the gift of the Eucharist, which is the wonder of the divine lover giving himself. Prayer is the way of doing this, and that is why prayer in our lives is so important. It seems fair to say that if we don't pray, we don't love God. Not praying is like never visiting someone we claim to love very much. But we also have to give God gifts, as we give to all we love. The gift he wants of us is a faithful life and a life of service, and a life of love for all his children.

How do we cultivate love of neighbor? We look at their good points, and forget their bad ones, as we want God to do for us. We find the generosity in our hearts to give to and serve them. We make it a point of honor to try to give more than we receive. If we want to love warmly we need to grow generous. Selfishness is a killer of love.

We put people above possessions. In the Wall Street crash of 1987, investors flocked to psychiatrists. Losing their money made them lose their sense of self-worth. They needed help to think through their values. One psychiatrist said that these people might begin to discover that their human relationships were worth a thousand times more than their money.

Sometimes we don't see the good in a person, and have to love him in faith, the way we love the God we can't see. That is a noble act of trust in God the Creator, and will be rewarded.

God has joined and bonded the two loves, our love of God and love of one another. What God has joined together, let no man put asunder. To understand this bond, picture the love in your heart as the sun. Its light and warmth go out to everyone. By withholding love from anyone, we harm our love for everyone, because our love is like God's, who loves all that he has made.

"ABC" — Feast of All Saints
Rv 7:2-4, 9-14
1 Jn 3:1-3
Mt 5:1-12

HOME TO THE FATHER

The year-end holidays are approaching. Families and clans will gather, friends will visit. We can see in such gatherings a dress rehearsal for the feast we celebrate today. When Cardinal Manning was dying, he was asked how he felt. "Like a school boy," he said, "going home for the holidays."

Today we celebrate the feast of the saints gathered in the home of the Father. In this instance, the reunion won't break up after the holidays. This homecoming is forever.

St. Paul once asked the following question: "Is it possible that he who did not spare his own Son but handed him over for the sake of us all will not grant us all things besides?" Today we celebrate God's answer. We can no more imagine the home the Father has prepared for us than a cave man could imagine a modern house, or a cave woman a modern kitchen.

This feast of All Saints is unique in the whole Church calendar. Other feast days celebrate others, but today we include ourselves. To rephrase a famous statement of Pogo, "We have met the saints and they are us." Granted, we aren't the finished product yet, but we have the call, and are in the process of completion. St.

Paul used to call Christians like us "the saints," so I am not presumptuous in saying this.

In the first reading we have John's futuristic vision of the saints gathered before the divine throne. God willing, we were among them. Today's feast invites us to realize that we have been called to be saints, that it is a call to live in holiness, and that it is fitting to celebrate our communion with all the saints.

First, we are all called to be saints. There is no exception. Once you grant that God became man to redeem us, it's unthinkable that he would do the job halfway. Jesus himself said, "You must become perfect as your heavenly Father is perfect." One little catechism asked the question, Can we be like God? It answered *Yes,* and quoted the very Scripture passage we have in today's second reading: "We shall be like him for we shall see him as he is." In view of these clear statements in God's word, it's not surprising that Vatican II taught that every single one of us is called to holiness.

What is holiness? It's what God is. Only God is holy. We can become holy only by sharing God's holiness. A chalice is made holy by consecration to God. We became consecrated to God by baptism. We were given sanctifying grace. We were made a new creation, given a share in the divine nature, made children and friends of God, given the Holy Spirit, and joined to the Church of Christ. By being sanctified in all these ways, we were given the vocation to be saints.

What is a saint? In the first reading John describes the saints as those who survived the great time of trial and washed their robes white in the Lamb's blood. In the second reading, he describes the saints as the little children of God who grew up and have now become full-fledged sons and daughter of God, like him, and with him, and seeing him. In the Gospel, Jesus describes the saints by the way they live, but we will come to that.

Second, we are called to live the holiness we've inherited. Holiness is the sure road to eternal life. In the beatitudes Jesus spells out the way to holiness. How many did you identify with? There is nothing in them we can't do or be. If we imitate Jesus, we will practice them all, for he *is* the beatitudes in the flesh. Just remember that God calls us to nothing we won't love if we give it a chance. Is there anyone who doesn't wish to be like Jesus? That's all the Father wants of any of us.

The highly attractive thing about the call to holiness is the call to be the great lover. Pope Paul VI said that what most identifies the uniqueness of a human being is his "capacity to love, to love to the end, to give himself with that love that is stronger than death and extends into eternity." He pointed to the martyrs as the sublime expression of this quality. Theirs was the noblest of all loves, not only in the way they gave, but in him to whom they gave it, the God who died for them.

Our way to holiness shares more with the martyrs than we realize. The word *martyr* means *witness*. To live a life of holiness is to give that witness to God in a kind of living martyrdom. In some ways that is harder. We feel at times that to be faithful to God we have to shed the very blood of our souls, and that it would be easier to lie down and die. Only our deep love for Christ sustains us on this journey into holiness.

Thirdly, it is fitting to hold a feast to what we are, God's family of saints. We, the family of God, are in three stages of progress. We are the Church militant on earth, the Church suffering in purgatory, and the Church triumphant in heaven. We are all for one, and one for all.

The saints in heaven strengthened our faith on earth by their lives, won merits that gain us graces, and pray for us still.

The saints in purgatory need our prayers and good works to win them release. We will remember them especially tomorrow on All Souls Day. They in turn will be interceding for us.

We on earth are still fighting the battles of love and faithfulness. We should never lose sight of the nobility of our struggle. It is the very likeness of Christ's. And we have a great cheering section in heaven, composed of the angels and saints. They must let out a great cry of joy every time one of us makes an end run around a temptation, and scores a touchdown of grace. One more for the Saints!

We have here the perfect banquet for our celebration. The Mass is both the memory of victory and its promise. It was first celebrated in tender love at the Last Supper and then offered in bloody triumph on Calvary. Since then, the pattern has been repeated. We offer it in the love of the Last Supper, then go out with the strength it gives us to win anew Calvary's victory over lovelessness and sin. That pattern is our march to the glory those before us have won.

Today is the day to remember life's bottom line and renew our resolve: We will live in the likeness of Christ to be there when the saints go marching in.

"A" — Thirty-first Sunday of the Year   Ml 1:14-2:2, 8-10
                                                1 Th 2:7-9, 13
                                                Mt 23:1-12

OVERCOMING OUR CRISIS OF FAITH

Through the prophet Malachi, God gives his priests more than an earful for their false teaching. They have thrown the faith of the people into crisis. We have a similar crisis of faith today.

The crisis is real. Joseph Cardinal Ratzinger, Prefect of the Office of the Faith, describes a crisis of faith, a crisis of the Church, a crisis of trust in dogma, a crisis of confidence in Scripture, and a crisis of morality. Priests, thelogians and lay people are detailing these crises, and we are all feeling them.

Malachi well describes our crisis. He says, "Have we not one Father? Has not the one God created us? Why then do we break faith with each other, violating the covenant of our fathers?''

Why indeed? What has brought on our crisis, what can we do about it, and what can we learn from the past to help?

What has brought on our crisis? We can trace it to many roots. We will consider the chief one here. The adaptations made by the Second Vatican Council of the Sixties disturbed the faith of some, and raised in others unreal and bizarre expectations of further change. The first group resists legitimate change, and the second produces illegitimate change.

Because the Church changed some of its Church-made laws such as fasting and abstinence and the language of the liturgy, Catholics began demanding changes in God's law on sexual morality and marriage and other matters. Priests and theologians willing to promote their cause appeared, and the confusion began. When sound theologians studied Catholic doctrine and applied it more currently to the problems of the day, they were attacked by the alarmed as though they were equally unfaithful.

To Pope John Paul II on his '87 visit, Cardinal Bernardin explained things this way: "When the Holy See reaffirms a teaching which has been part of our heritage for centuries . . . it is sometimes accused . . . of making new and unreasonable impositions on the people. In like manner, when someone questions how a truth might be better articulated or lived today, he or she is sometimes accused of rejecting the truth itself or portrayed as being in conflict with the Church's teaching authority."

What can we do about dissension in the Church? Everyone has to learn that there has always been development of doctrine in the Church. And that mistakes are made. But if the mistake-makers are obstinate, heresy and division follow. The third letter of John tells us that "Anyone so 'progressive' as not to remain in the teaching of Jesus Christ does not have God."

Therefore, while development is important, holding to the substance of the faith is the most crucial of all. Surely, the Spirit of God who guided Malachi is warning us to stop turning aside from

God's teaching. Many priests and people are following the opinions of favorite theologians against the official teaching of the Church.

That contrary teaching is called dissent. Contrast it with today's Gospel. Jesus commands obedience to religious leaders. And he tells his followers high and low not to be teachers of their own doctrine, but messengers who pass on his: "One among you is your teacher, the rest are learners," he says, and adds, "Avoid being called teachers. Only one is your teacher, the Messiah." St. Paul obeyed. He says he preached "God's good tidings" which believers received "not as the word of men, but as it truly is, the word of God."

We all need Paul's awareness that revelation is not man's word but God's. It demands the utmost respect. Paul told the Galatians that he did not learn his Gospel from man, but received it as a revelation from Jesus Christ.

We need as well both Paul's humility and his reverence for the Church. When his doctrine was attacked, he didn't stand on his high horse. He went to Jerusalem. He laid his teaching before the other apostles "so that I might not be running," he explains, "or have run, in vain." Behold an apostle who mistrusted his doctrine until the Church approved of it. Here is the principle of orthodoxy, which is at the heart of the Church's nature. Orthodoxy is holding to the authentic faith as interpreted by the successors of the apostles. If priests and people followed Paul's example, would not dissension dissolve like a morning cloud?

When Pope John Paul II came to the U.S. in '87, he said that in the Church "theological discussion takes place within the framework of faith. Dissent from church doctrine remains what it is, dissent; as such it may not be proposed or received on an equal footing with the Church's authentic teaching." He called for sound catechetics for our children. He directed bishops to see that sound doctrine is taught in our colleges. He said that even this is not enough. There must be faith and prayer.

What can we learn from the past? Dispute and dissension in other ages sometimes ended in heresy and division, and sometimes peacefully. When dissension was grave and critical, the dispute was always resolved at the top, by the bishops of the world, with the successor of Peter at their head, as the Lord willed.

The crucial thing is to preserve orthodoxy without shutting out growing understanding of the faith, and its application to our developing culture and its new questions. That is what the Second Vatican Council was about. Orthodoxy is not static. It is the tradition applied to new needs without loss of substance. Anyone can contribute to development of doctrine, but only the whole Church guided by the Holy Spirit through the pope, or pope and bishops, can make a final determination of what is orthodox.

John Henry Cardinal Newman learned this so well it drew him from Anglicanism to Catholicism. His *Essay on the Development of Christian Doctrine* remains the valid groundwork for dealing with this issue, though he wrote it when he was still an Anglican.

The signs of the times call us to earnest prayer and faith, and reverent submission to the teaching Church. Such submission is necessary for the love of Christ and his body the Church, and for our own salvation. Have we not one God and Father? Why do we break faith with each other, violating the covenant of our fathers with Christ the Messiah and Son of God?

"A" — Thirty-second Sunday of the Year

Ws 6:12-16
1 Th 4:13-17
Mt 25:1-13

HOW TO PREPARE FOR DEATH

By faith, the Jewish people have learned to laugh at their fears and troubles even as they cry. They tell the story of a weary old man who throws down the bundle of sticks he is carrying and shouts, "O Angel of Death, where are you?" An angel of fearsome aspect appears and asks, "Did you call me? What do you want?" The terrified old man mumbles, "I just wanted you to help me put this bundle back on my shoulders."

As we near the end of the liturgical year, the Church puts before us mortals death and eternal life. Unfortunately, most of us have toward death that double-mindedness the old man shows. We want the promised life, yet fear the passage of death. But God's word helps us stir our desire, and put down our fear.

To better absorb God's word, and better prepare for that inevitable moment, let's ponder three questions: What is more important than dying well? What are the obstacles to dying well? How can we prepare to die well?

First, what is more important than dying well? Jesus is impelling us to ask that question by his parable. He will either call us to him by our individual deaths, or return suddenly to us all. St. Paul assures us that one way has no advantage over the other, for at Christ's Second Coming the dead will rise at once.

Either way, when he comes, our lamp of love must be burning. If the gales of our sins put it out before that, we have time to repent and ask forgiveness. But for one who crosses the Great Divide with the lamp out, time has run out.

Love is the lamp that must be burning. St. John of the Cross says that in the evening of life we will be examined in love. Is our love of God and neighbor burning bright? With what do you feed the flame? What is this oil that burns in the lamp of love? Some say it's faith. It must include faith, for the Scriptures tell us that without faith we cannot please God. St. Catherine of Siena said it is humility — for without humility love dies. The oil of our baptismal anointing is in it too. And the mixture must include good deeds, for love takes no vacations. Do you ever let a day go by without doing a good deed to feed the lamp of love?

If we don't die well, all is lost. Many parishes used to have a

"Happy Death Society." To a pagan that's a contradiction in terms, but not to us. We anticipate risen bodies surging with life. We look forward to living in our Father's house forever. Even if we fear a little because our faith is shaky and our lives shakier, we have cause to look to death with joy. Our Lord won't fail us if only we are sincerely trying to do his will.

What are the obstacles to dying well? The only real obstacle is not living well. People die as they live. Five bridesmaids did not live well. Jesus doesn't want us to make their mistake.

To live well, we need wisdom. The first reading assures us that wisdom is most eager to be found. When you find her, you will know her by her loveliness. She is cloaked in the beauty of truth; she radiates peace and joy. She is full of love and most concerned for our welfare. She frees us from care, for she trains us to do what we ought, and leave the rest confidently to God. But how find her? She invites us to keep vigil by prayer in the night and by rising to pray in the morning. Since that is wise, in doing it we are already finding her. And in prayer we find her the more, for wisdom is none other than God.

Another obstacle to dying well is fear that God doesn't love you. Of this I can assure you, that God loves you. We need not be concerned about that, but we must be concerned about whether we love God. Only those who love him can live in his home.

How shall we prepare to die well? By living well. In the opening prayer we asked God for health in mind and body to do his work on earth. That is what he wants of us. If we live the faith, and carry out the duties of our state of life, we will die well.

We prepare by getting the work done God wants us to do. At the Last Supper, Jesus said to the Father, "I have glorified you on earth. I have finished the work you gave me to do." Say that to the Father yourself just for the sound of it. Then pray him to help you so to live that one day you can say it with the joy Jesus had when he said it. Look your life over, and see if you are omitting any of the work he wants of you, so you can get to it.

We prepare for death by dying to self long before the Angel of Death comes calling. In the opening prayer we pray for freedom of spirit. It's amazing how free we can be of earth's hold once we know we are really pleasing God by our lives day in and day out. As we please God, and know he takes pleasure in us, we take more and more pleasure in him. Then we can say in all honesty, "For you my flesh pines and my soul thirsts." And we may even find we can say, "I will remember you on my couch, and through the night watches I will meditate on you."

We prepare for death by realizing, as St. Ambrose says, that God prescribed death as a remedy for sin. It is a medicine we needn't fear, for the Good Physician has prescribed the dose for our sakes. We don't know how long it will be before Jesus returns. But we know that if he delays too long, he won't make us wait, but will call us home through the door of death, as he has so many of his saints before us. How surprised we will be when we see how kind and beautiful the Angel of Death really is.

We prepare for death by asking for the prayers of the saints, and most of all, of our Blessed Mother. Over and over, we say to Holy Mary, "Pray for us sinners now and at the hour of our death."

We prepare for death by meditating on Jesus dying on the cross. He died and rose for us. We will die and rise for him. And if in meditation we spend time with him in his hour of death, do you think he and the Blessed Mother won't be with us in ours?

We remain always prepared by receiving the Sacrament of Reconciliation often, and at once if we fall into serious sin. We make an act of contrition each night, not to be caught unawares. When we are sick in bed, we call a priest.

Christ has come. Christ is coming to us in the Eucharist. Christ will come again to take us home. Let us give him and ourselves endless joy by being ready.

THE MANDATE TO EXCEL

A Jewish man went to his rabbi and demanded to know why God distributes his gifts so unequally. The rabbi whispered, ''Not so loud. God might hear you and say, 'If you're anxious to know, come up here and find out.' '' That is wise advice.

Unlike the lazy lout in today's parable, we should question not the master's conduct but our own. We are one week from the end of the Liturgical Year, which goes through the cycle of our Lord's life, and our own. So, in the Gospel, Jesus is inviting us to a dress rehearsal of the Last Judgment. He wants us to take stock of our lives before the final curtain comes down.

How am I doing with my gifts and talents? The *Wall Street Journal* reported that more business people fail because of poor record keeping than for any other reason. They think they're O.K. when in comes an unexpected bill, and crash! They're bankrupt.

The same sort of thing happens in life with God. Some people think they're in good spiritual shape, when in fact they have nothing in their heavenly bank account of good deeds. All they consider is the sins they haven't committed, like a penniless business man bragging about not having any unpaid bills. Then in comes the bill for forgotten sins, or for the grievous wrongs approved of in their own minds, but not in God's, and crash, they're bankrupt. How do they differ from the lazy lout of Jesus' parable who had no profit and thought he had done no wrong?

What will the Lord look for at the Last Judgment? How does this guide our daily life? How does our life differ from the good unbeliever's?

First, then, what will the Lord look for at the Last Judgment? Today's parable tells us. Christ has mandated us to excel. He will look to see how we did with the lot or the little we had. He calls us not only to be good, but to be good at doing good. God gave us our gifts for use.

The Second Vatican Council was like a commentary on today's parable. In uncounted ways it told us to develop and use our intellectual, spiritual and social talents in the service of God and man. It called us to work harder on earth than those who don't believe in heaven. We owe it to God and his plan for creation. We owe it to Christ and his people in need. Inactive Christians are useless, just like the man in today's parable. Neither God nor man admires the "good" man who does little good. Like Jesus, we must not just be good, but go around doing good.

At the Last Judgment God will look at how well we developed and used all he gave us for the good of all. We'll all have sins to account for, but Scripture assures us that doing good to others, especially spiritual good, makes up for a lot of sins.

We can't be so fearful of doing wrong that we do nothing. The lout in the parable spent his time harshly judging his master instead of working hard to earn a favorable judgment from him.

Too many people view morality and religion as a set of rules about what not to do. That's the least part of both. Their main purpose is to help us develop the virtues and qualities that make us good, make us able to do good, and make us doers of good. How can we miss the point when Christ's emphasis is always on love? We take it for granted that love does no evil. What we look for is love that does good. By that we judge it, and so does God. What saint was sainted just for staying out of sin?

Secondly, how does this guide our daily life? Children are called to be good students, to make something of themselves, so that they can grow up as reliable and productive persons. They are called to work hard at their religious education and formation, for it will be the guide of their lives. Given half a chance, they should go on to higher education. Employed people are called to be competent, industrious and reliable, so as to help provide the products people need, and be a credit to their Catholic faith.

The home is central to it all. The first reading praises the good wife and mother. It describes the beauty of her soul and her life. It never mentions her appearance, but you could draw up a lovely list of her virtues. They should remind us of Mary.

Husband and wife are called to develop and radiate the image and likeness of God. Their love expresses Christ's loving union with his Church. They share Christ's mission of giving life. They share his prophetic mission by forming their children in the faith. They share his royal priesthood by consecrating their home life to godlikeness. By working industriously and managing well they exercise Christ's kingly rule over their own little domain. They are found at Mass faithfully, and are known to share in the works of the parish, and to contribute what they can to charity. They exercise their love and respect for life and goodness and concern for others by their participation in the political life of the nation. These common but priceless ways and means of life are what Christ asks, and will look for at the end time.

Thirdly, how should we differ from the good unbeliever? We should have a far wider focus and commitment. A good unbeliever, at best, is concerned for people's good on earth. We are concerned as well for their eternal good. Our faith, our prayer, and our lives should deny what is, in the end, the hopelessness of the unbeliever. Even without words, our way of life should say to all, ''We were all made to enter into the joy of the Lord.''

We can also bear with the suffering and unequal distribution of gifts that make unbelievers despair. We expect surprises at the Last Judgment. We know God expects from the less gifted, the handicapped and the suffering only what they can give. Jesus said the poor widow who gave her last few cents gave more than all the wealthy. We know that some whom others judge useless and put last will be put first by God for excelling in doing much with little, and in uncomplainingly bearing the cross with Jesus, like Simon of Cyrene. But we never use that as an excuse for not helping.

We all share the greatest talent of all, which is to become mature sons and daughters of God. That's what God wants to see and embrace at the Last Judgment. He will be waiting anxiously to find us worthy, so that he can give us the final and the greatest gift, himself.

"A" — Thirty-fourth Sunday of the Year

Ezk 34:11-12, 15-17
1 Cor 15:20-26, 28
Mt 25:31-46

OUR KING'S LAW OF LOVE

"My fellow Americans," President John F. Kennedy said in his inaugural address, "Ask not what your country can do for you. Ask what you can do for your country." Ages before him, our great Lord and King said something similar, as we heard in today's Gospel. It's not enough to have faith in what God can do for us; we must have the faithfulness to do what we can for him.

Today, we are lifted out of time and space and, as though seeing through the eyes of God, are given a preview of the General Judgment, the closing drama of salvation history.

Some of the favorite textbooks of many children are those math books which have the answers in the back. They can keep working until they get the right answer. That's the kind of help our Lord is giving us. He provides the right answers to the questions on our final exam, so we can get it right. Jesus has no wish to spring a trap on us. He tells us exactly what he wants. How grateful we should be to have such a king.

The ancients thought of their gods as capricious, immoral and unjust. Only the revelation that came from God through the Jewish people, and finally through Christ, set us straight. It reveals God's love for us, and his faithfulness and mercy, and also his justice. That is the theme we celebrate today.

Recall the history of peoples governed by bloody and unjust kings. Then rejoice in Christ our King. The conqueror Napoleon himself made a comparison between the warlords of history and our King of kings. He said that Alexander the Great, Caesar, Charlemagne and he himself had founded far-reaching empires, but that they depended on force. He contrasted this with Jesus, who founded love's kingdom. Jesus demands the unconditional love of the heart, he said, and his demand is granted, though fathers ask it in vain of their children, and brides of their spouses, and brother of brother. To this day, he said, millions are ready to die for him. "Time, the great destroyer," he went on, "is powerless to extinguish the sacred flame." And he added, "This it is which proves to me the divinity of Christ."

In the first reading today, we have God promising his coming hundreds of years before the birth of Christ. "I myself will look after and tend my sheep," he says. We can only appreciate what God is saying if we get rid of the romantic notion of shepherds. They were dirty, unkempt, poor laborers in the fields, often despised by the more affluent. Yet that didn't put God off. That is what he was going to become for love of us all. Today's psalm of the Lord as shepherd expresses the trust, confidence, love and gratitude that we should have for so good a king and shepherd.

In the second reading, Paul summarizes what our Victor-King is doing for us. He is the great power over all powers, the authority over all authorities. Our great King strides forth and conquers even death. How privileged we are to have him. How good of him to be this for us. He is leading us back to the Father.

Now we look at today's gravely important Gospel. It's a dress rehearsal for the Final Judgment. It gives us the answers we must have ready. It expresses Christ's great love, and great appreciation

of our love. It also expresses his justice. A king must be just, or
what good is he to people treated unjustly?

Did you note that sin is not mentioned in the Final Judgment,
nor worship, nor the word *love*? Only deeds are mentioned, deeds
of love. St. Ignatius said, "Love ought to manifest itself in deeds
rather than in words." St. John of the Cross said, "In the evening
of life, we will be examined in love." Isn't this an examination in
love? Out of the keeping of the commandments, out of our worship, should come deeds of love. To them we are called, and on
them, judged.

One young priest told how shocked he was on hearing confes-
sions: shocked not by what he heard, but by what he didn't hear. He
found people examining their consciences like immature children,
and not according to this final exam. Do we confess only what we
do, or also what we fail to do? Do we give our hands as well as our
hearts to the service of Christ and his people?

As priests are supposed to serve the body of Christ in its
spiritual needs, lay people are supposed to serve its material needs.
We are his body, and must serve one another as his body. Christ
will say, "As often as you did it for one of my least brothers, you
did it for me" — or failed to do it. God loves us body and soul; he's
concerned for us on earth as well as in heaven, in time as well as in
eternity. Our parish carries on many good services for Christ.
Make sure you are a part of them, so you will pass the final exam
with flying colors.

We will be helped by pondering the great kindness of our
King. So loving is he that he wants the naked clothed, the hungry
fed, the homeless sheltered, the sick visited, the imprisoned to
know they are loved. He wants *want* done away with. St. Gregory
of Nazianzen said, "Resolve to imitate God's justice, and no one
will be poor." To incite us to love, Jesus has promised such great
rewards that you'd think we'd be standing in line to serve the poor,
instead of them standing in line looking for help. No wonder Mary
and all the saints were so eager to help everyone.

Today, in Holy Communion with our loving King, let us each pledge to him our hands and our hearts. But first, let us do it together. I invite you to say after me the prayer of consecration to the King of the Universe. The prayer gains us a plenary indulgence if we add prayers for the Holy Father, and confess and receive Communion within three weeks. Here is the prayer:

O Lord Jesus, I acknowledge you King of the universe. All that has been created has been made for you. Make full use of your rights over me. I renew my baptismal promises renouncing Satan and all his works and pomps. I promise to live a good Christian life and to do all in my power to bring about the triumph of the rights of God and your Church. Divine Heart of Jesus, I offer you my efforts so that all hearts may acknowledge your sacred kingship and thus the kingdom of your peace may be established in the whole world. Amen.